A New Way to Live with Loss

Grief medicine through animal wisdom and numerology

Amanda Lee

HEMBURY
—BOOKS—

Copyright © Amanda Lee
First published by Hembury Books in 2025
hemburybooks.com.au
info@hemburybooks.com

Hardback ISBN 9781923517455
Paperback ISBN 9781923517448
Ebook ISBN 9781923517431

The moral right of the author has been asserted.
All rights reserved. No portion of this book may be reproduced in any form without permission from the author and publisher, except as permitted by Australian copyright law.

 A catalogue record for this book is available from the National Library of Australia

You can connect with Amanda Lee via:
Web | www.blazecoaches.com
Email | amanda@blazecoaches.com

Or on social media
Instagram | amandalee_author
LinkedIn | Amanda-lee888
Facebook | BlazeCoaching

To my Dad, Roger, this first one is for you.

And I know you know, but when I finally got around
to reading *that* book we spoke about, well,
the Universe opened up and
it just all clicked into place.
Despite that, I still miss you.

Love always,
Amanda Jane
xoxo

Contents

About the Author 7
Acknowledgement of Wisdom Keepers 9
Foreword 10
Introduction 12
Animal wisdom & daily practices 26

    1 Eagle 30
    2 Hawk 34
    3 Elk 38
    4 Deer 42
    5 Bear 46
    6 Snake 50
    7 Skunk 54
    8 Otter 58
    9 Butterfly 62
  10 Turtle 66
  11 Moose 70
  12 Porcupine 74
  13 Coyote 78
  14 Dog 82
  15 Wolf 86
  16 Raven 90
  17 Mountain Lion 94
  18 Lynx 98
  19 Buffalo 102
  20 Mouse 106
  21 Owl 110
  22 Beaver 114
  23 Opossum 118
  24 Crow 121
  25 Fox 125

26	Squirrel	128
27	Dragonfly	132
28	Armadillo	136
29	Badger	140
30	Rabbit	144
31	Turkey	148
32	Ant	152
33	Weasel	156
34	Grouse	160
35	Horse	163
36	Lizard	168
37	Antelope	172
38	Frog	175
39	Swan	179
40	Dolphin	183
41	Whale	188
42	Bat	193
43	Spider	197
44	Hummingbird	201
45	Blue Heron	205
46	Raccoon	209
47	Prairie Dog	213
48	Wild Boar	217
49	Salmon	221
50	Alligator	225
51	Jaguar	229
52	Black Panther	233
53	Lioness	237
54	Elephant	241
55	Bee	245
56	Tiger	249

Index on Pythagorean Numbers & Animals 253
Cultural and Source Acknowledgement 257

A compassionate guide to navigating loss, meaning-making, and personal growth by blending timeless wisdom with practical reflection tools.

Hope | Help | Healing
Blaze Coaching – Light the fire within

ABOUT THE AUTHOR

Amanda Lee writes from a place where grief is understood as a force which requires our attention but not our submission. As both a writer and the founder of Blaze Coaching and the Cope Better Foundation and having experienced a quick succession of familial losses herself, Amanda is dedicated to changing how grief is understood and supported around the world.

A New Way to Live With Loss is Amanda's heartfelt offering to anyone seeking guidance, meaning or simply a companion through grief. Broken into chapters symbolised by a number, animal spirit and emotional theme, Amanda's book invites readers to explore a holistic form of healing rooted in symbolism, self-awareness, gentle transformation and most importantly, hope.

With a background in corporate leadership and a deep personal connection to healing work, Amanda brings a unique blend of professionalism and compassion to everything she does. Her work integrates tools from grief recovery methodology, animal archetypes, Pythagorean numerology and emotional wellbeing practices to support people through life's most challenging transitions.

Growing up, Amanda's favourite animal was the whale and she would constantly regale her adult audience with the dimensions and attributes of all species of the marine mammal. As she grew older, she was drawn to the grey wolf - a symbol of guidance and collective strength, and marking a new chapter in her life centred on leadership and teaching, which continues today.

ACKNOWLEDGEMENT OF WISDOM KEEPERS

This work stands on the shoulders of many who have carried sacred knowledge through stories and lived experience. Amanda honours the cultures, elders, lineages and authors who have shared animal wisdom across time - from Dreaming stories and ancestral teachings to sacred texts and contemporary works like *Animal Medicine Cards* by Jamie Sams and David Carson and a giant in this field, Ted Andrews with *Animal Speak*.

Other wonderful teachers also include her Numerology and Reiki teacher, Deb Bull of Soul Evolution, Scott Alexander King of *Animal Dreaming* in Australia, Dan Millman's brilliant work on numerology – *The Life You were Born to Live*, and her wonderful clients that have trusted her with their journey.

Her intention is not to recreate or speak for these traditions, but to reflect what they have offered her as a coach and fellow human navigating grief. With deep respect and gratitude, she acknowledges all those who walk the path of wisdom-sharing and healing.

FOREWORD

A baby crow crash-landed into my window the other day and became wedged between it and the couch. I ran to free the bird who, bewildered and unsure, managed to stumble to his feet. Let's call him Charlie.

I followed Charlie's progress as he took up temporary residence in my yard. On day one, he cautiously made his way up a small but unstable tree where he perched for 24 hours. Gusty winds threatened to topple him, but he was resilient and held on. On the second day, Charlie slowly made his way to a stronger tree. He seemed settled there, fluffing his wings around his small body, but was still unsure of flight. With the next morning's dawning sun, Charlie miraculously found his wings and flew away. I was overjoyed, but it was only in his leaving that I realised how significant Charlie was.

I was asked to write a foreword for this book only days before Charlie arrived. He showed me the way. The power of animal magic! With grief, we often crash-land and are left feeling dazed and stunned. All we can do is try fiercely to hold on as the winds of grief and loss thrash around us.

This book aims to provide stable branches for you to grasp as the healing process takes place. It will give you the tools and awareness so that you too can eventually fly again. This book is for anybody with the willingness to find the path out of grief towards awareness, resilience and strength.

With courage and openness, Amanda will lead you through the throes of grief. Her words are a testament to the strength that can be found in the signs all around us and demonstrate a deep understanding of numerology and animal wisdom which informs her empathetic worldview. This is more than a book; it is the mighty tree which will provide comfort and stability as you move, gain awareness and heal at your own pace. Just like Charlie.

— **Deb Bull**, Founder of Soul Evolution, Healer, Teacher and Pythagorean Numerology Expert

INTRODUCTION

Thank you for allowing me to join you on your grief recovery journey.

Grief is a deeply personal and transformative journey, often leaving us feeling adrift in a sea of emotions.

In 2007, my dad and maternal grandparents all passed between January to May. The following year, my dad's parents also passed, and I left my husband. I acutely learned the impacts of grief, both through death and living loss.

The pain of loss can be overwhelming, and in those moments, many of us seek guidance and support through spiritual or traditional practices. One powerful source of wisdom comes from animal medicine, which holds that animals embody energies and teachings that can assist in our healing.

Across cultures, animals have long carried profound meaning, representing strength, protection, guidance, and transformation. I've always been drawn to this symbolism. Whether it's a Wolf showing us a new path or a Raven inviting us to embrace mystery, these spirits remind us that we are not alone. Healing can come from nature, from stories, and from the quiet, yet persistent ways the Universe communicates when we are ready to listen.

During my own experience, I found solace through the gentle messages of these animal guides. I used Scott Alexander King meditations to invite animals into my conscious awareness, helping me face one of the strongest emotions I could not shake – sadness. A Mountain Lion appeared for me, becoming a close companion on my journey to healing.

From that time forward, I introduced animal medicine into my grief recovery work, and the impact was profound. People who had been stuck in their grief began to move forward, whether the loss was through death, separation, dementia, illness, or other life changes. Connecting with the spirit of these animals provides insight and strength, helping us navigate the complex landscape of grief and offering a path toward understanding, acceptance, and renewal.

With openness and courage, many have embraced their own animal guides and set out on a new path. I hope this book can offer the same guidance. It combines the ancient practice of animal medicine with the timeless wisdom of Pythagorean numerology, creating a holistic approach to healing that nurtures mind, body, and spirit — a framework that aligns closely with cognitive behaviour therapy, one of my favourite coaching tools.

I would like to recognise the individual and collective expertise of those with a living or lived experience of a mental health condition, or those that are grieving. We pay tribute to the vital contribution to system change and recognise the courage shown in sharing this unique perspective, one that provides hope and shapes a better future for themselves and others.

How to use this book

This book is designed to be a companion on your grief journey, offering insights, tools, and practices to help you navigate loss with greater understanding and self-compassion. It blends ancient wisdom with modern life coaching approaches, including techniques drawn from

Neuro-Linguistic Programming (NLP) and Cognitive Behavioural Therapy (CBT). These evidence-based methods support emotional regulation, reframing of thought patterns, and the development of practical coping strategies to sustain you through different phases of grief.

Chapters are organised by numbers, each aligned with Pythagorean numerology, allowing you to explore the unique energy associated with each animal and number combination. Through stories and practical guidance, each animal invites you to explore its symbolic qualities and their relevance to your personal journey of loss and healing.

You can use this book in several ways:

- Shuffle the card deck, and allow the Universe to guide you in selecting an animal and corresponding number to support you for the day, month, or year. Read the relevant page and reflect on how the questions and fables resonate with you. You may select multiple cards in a day.
- Read it sequentially, allowing each chapter to build upon the last as you explore deeper aspects of your grief.
- Choose a chapter based on your emotional state or current need, finding the animal spirit that aligns with your feelings in that moment.
- If you have a favourite number, or a special anniversary date for remembrance, the corresponding number for that animal may serve as a meaningful guide - turn to that page and see what insights it offers.
- Apply the Triangle Effect™, integrating your thoughts, emotions, and behaviours to create a balanced and holistic response to your grief experience. Begin by sitting quietly and shuffling the card deck with intention, allowing yourself to breathe deeply and

settle into the present moment. When you feel ready, draw three cards. Lay them out in the shape of a triangle:

- **Top of the triangle – Thoughts:** This animal represents the mental patterns, narratives, or perspectives currently shaping your experience. Reflect on what beliefs or insights it brings to light.
- **Bottom left – Emotions/Feelings:** This animal connects you with your emotional landscape. Notice how the animal's qualities speak to your inner world and feelings that may need acknowledgment or expression.
- **Bottom right – Actions/Behaviours:** This animal highlights action, movement, or conscious choice. Consider what practical or symbolic steps this animal suggests, remembering that action can also mean active reflection or creating space for change.

Reflect on the relationship between the three points. The aim is to bring them into alignment, so that your inner world and outward expression work together in support of healing.

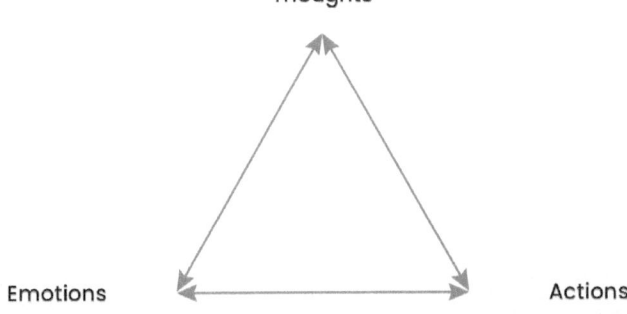

- Create your own Grief Map, using journalling prompts, reflective questions, and numerology insights to chart your progress, identify patterns, and develop personalised strategies for healing over time. Begin by sitting quietly and shuffling the deck. When ready, draw five cards, laying them out in a structured pattern:
    - **Centre – You, right now:** This card represents your current state, emotions, and inner energy.
    - **Below – Underlying issue:** Place a card beneath the centre. It reveals what may be unresolved or keeping you stuck beneath the surface.
    - **Above – Hidden perspective:** Place a card above the centre. This offers insight into what you may not be seeing - guidance or strength that can support your growth and help you move forward.
    - **Left – Feminine energy:** Place a card to the left. This speaks to your nurturing, intuitive, and restorative needs - what will support and soothe your spirit.
    - **Right – Masculine energy:** Place a card to the right. This represents purposeful action, clarity, or structure that can help propel you forward. Action may involve doing, but it can equally mean focused contemplation or setting clear intentions.

Take time to reflect on the spread as a whole. Journal what arises for each position, noticing patterns, contrasts, or messages that resonate. Your Grief Map becomes a visual and symbolic tool to understand where you are, what undercurrents influence your journey, and what supports are available to you as you navigate grief with both softness and strength.

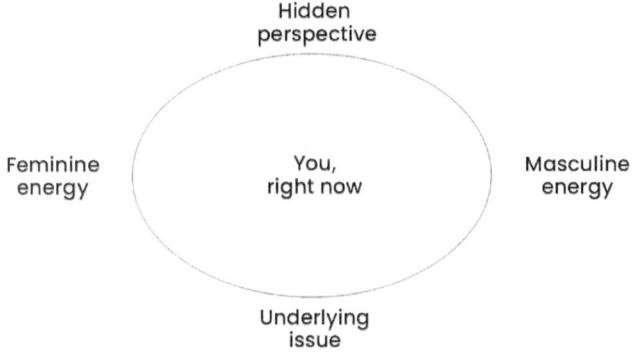

The History and Power of Pythagoras and Numerology

Pythagoras, the ancient Greek philosopher and mathematician (c. 570 – 495 BCE), is credited with developing the early foundations of numerology, though his contributions went beyond mathematics. Known for the Pythagorean Theorem, Pythagoras also believed that numbers held deep, mystical significance.

He founded a school of thought that viewed the Universe as interconnected through numbers and patterns, promoting the idea that the study of numbers could unlock the secrets of life and the cosmos. He believed in the vibrational power of numbers, asserting that they influence everything from music and geometry to personal traits and destiny.

How it works

In Pythagorean numerology, each letter in the alphabet is assigned a numerical value, and these values can be used to calculate a person's Life Path Number or other significant numbers. Each number, from 1 to 9, as well as the "Master Numbers" 11, 22, 33, 44 and 55, holds unique attributes that reflect character traits, challenges, and opportunities.

For example:

1. **Number 1:** Leadership, independence, confidence / self-doubt and vulnerability
2. **Number 3:** Creativity, expression, communication / blocked expression, lack of joy, negativity
3. **Number 8:** Power, abundance, generosity / self-worth, disempowerment, material focus

Pythagorean numerology continues to be influential today, especially in holistic and metaphysical practices, providing a framework for self-reflection, personal development, and spiritual alignment.

Note: this book does not focus on uncovering your personal numerology profile. You can find several wonderful websites that can assist you in this process and I would highly recommend Felicia Bender the Practical Numerologist: *https://feliciabender.com*.

Using numbers for your healing

In this book, numerology can be explored on a limited personal level, using the numbers from your date of birth and name, or on a Universal level, which is drawn from the date itself.

To calculate, simply add the numbers together until you reach a single digit.

- For example, 2025 becomes 2 + 0 + 2 + 5 = 9, making it a Universal 9 year – a time of endings, compassion, and forgiveness.
- If the 17th is significant to you, 1 + 7 = 8.
- A number like 10 reduces to 1 (1 + 0).
- A single number, such as 4, remains as it is.

The exceptions are 11, 22, 33, 44 and 55, known as Master numbers, which carry their own significance.

For some people, anniversary dates often hold special meaning, so while calendar days stop at 31, numbers beyond this can appear in your life through age, milestones, or recurring patterns, each holding special meaning.

You may be drawn to certain numbers for guidance, or you may connect with them through the animals in this book. For example, many people regard 33 as quite mystical, relating it to the age Jesus Christ was when he died. Similarly, the day of someone's passing, or major life event often holds significance.

The animals in this book reach the number 56, allowing several ways for you to connect to numerology and learn more about the energy associated with each number.

The Ancient Teachings of Animals: Universal Wisdom Across Cultures

Throughout history, animals have been revered for their ability to convey spiritual lessons and offer guidance. Long before organised religion, many societies practised animism - the belief that all elements of the natural world, including animals, plants, rivers, and mountains, possess a living spirit. Within these communities, animals were regarded as teachers, protectors, guides and intermediaries between the human and spiritual realms. Their behaviours, movements, and appearances were interpreted as messages, offering direction, healing, and insight to those willing to observe with reverence.

This deep connection to the natural world is echoed across continents and cultures. In Indigenous traditions, animals often play central roles in creation stories and serve as clan totems or spiritual guides. Similarly, in ancient Celtic, Norse, African, and Asian spiritual systems, animals were seen as carriers of universal wisdom, reflecting human qualities and the rhythms of life.

One striking example is the ancient Bön religion of Tibet, which predates the arrival of Buddhism in the region around the 7th century CE. Bön is rooted in shamanic and animistic practices, honouring the spirits of the land, sky, and animals. Practitioners sought harmony between human life and the natural world, drawing upon the symbolic power of animals to understand both earthly and spiritual dimensions. When Buddhism later entered Tibet, many Bön practices were integrated into the evolving spiritual landscape, but the reverence for animals as messengers and guides remained. Travelling to Tibet many years ago was an experience like no other. Witnessing the assimilation of these two religions in a unique way through attending a sky burial site, sitting atop a mystical and revered white yak at Lake Namsto and meeting a man mourning his wife during the Year of the Sheep and inviting me to walk with him on his kora around the lake. A kora is a circular pilgrimage around a sacred site, object, or area, and is a fundamental part of Tibetan Buddhism and other religions in the region.

This universal respect for animals appears in myths and spiritual practices worldwide, revealing a shared human impulse to find meaning and guidance in the living world. Animals transcend language and culture; their symbolism offers timeless insights into human behaviour, emotional resilience, and spiritual growth.

✣ Native American Traditions

In Native American cultures, animals are often seen as spirit guides or totems, embodying specific qualities that individuals can learn from. For instance, the wolf is revered for its leadership, and pack instinct, while the bear represents strength and introspection. Each animal carries a unique medicine, teaching people about their character traits, strengths, and areas of personal growth. Native American teachings focus on the interconnectedness of all life, with animals serving as both teachers and guardians.

✳ Ancient Egyptian Symbolism

In ancient Egypt, animals were seen as sacred beings linked to the Gods. The falcon was connected to Horus and stood for protection and divine authority. The cat, associated with Bastet, was honoured as a guardian of the home and a symbol of fertility. Many animals were believed to carry divine power, and their images appeared alongside deities to express the qualities they embodied. This reflected the Egyptian view that animals held a wisdom that connected the human and spiritual realms.

✳ Hindu and Buddhist Traditions

In Hinduism and Buddhism, animals hold sacred meaning and often embody divine qualities. The cow is honoured as a symbol of life and nourishment, central to spiritual practice. The elephant, through the God Ganesha, represents wisdom and the power to clear obstacles. In Buddhist teachings, the tiger embodies protection, while the deer reflects peace and gentle awareness. Across these traditions, animals remind humans of their bond with all living beings and the importance of living with compassion.

✳ Celtic Mythology

In Celtic culture, animals carried profound symbolic weight and were often linked to the mysteries of life and the unseen. The raven was seen as a creature of prophecy, bringing messages of change. The stag, with its rising antlers, signified spiritual authority and a bridge to the Otherworld. The boar was revered for its courage and ferocity, inspiring strength in those who faced great challenges. For the Celts, animals were not simply symbols but companions on life's path, guiding and protecting through both the ordinary and the sacred.

✻ Norse Mythology

In Norse mythology, animals are woven into the fabric of fate and often appear as signs of what lies ahead. Ravens were sacred to Odin for their ability to travel between worlds and carry hidden knowledge. Wolves could be seen as loyal protectors, yet also as forces of chaos in figures like Fenrir. Serpents appeared in stories of endings and renewal, holding immense power in their presence. These animals were more than symbols; they reflected the untamed forces of existence that humans had to face.

✻ Aboriginal Australians

In Aboriginal Australian cultures, animals are sacred beings woven into the Dreaming, the spiritual framework that unites people with the land and their ancestors. Each person may belong to a totem animal, experienced as a living relationship rather than a symbol. A totem shapes kinship and obligations, while also deepening connection to Country. In times of grief, turning to one's totem or noticing animal messengers in nature can bring grounding and a sense of ancestral presence.

✻ African Traditional Beliefs

Across many African traditions, animals are deeply connected to the spirit realm. They may act as messengers, protectors, or manifestations of deities and ancestors. The lioness can signify courage and leadership, while the snake represents transformation or ancestral warning. In ceremonies, animal energies are invoked through music, dance, or divination to guide healing, resolve grief, and restore balance between the living and the spirit world.

✲ Shinto (Japan)

Shinto honours *kami*, the sacred spirits that inhabit natural elements, including animals. The fox, as a messenger of the deity Inari, symbolises intuition and protection, while cranes are associated with longevity and spiritual blessings. In grief, offerings such as rice products and sake, and quiet rituals at shrines help maintain a connection with lost loved ones through the natural and animal world, affirming that spirits continue to exist within and around us.

✲ Māori (Aotearoa / New Zealand)

For the Māori, animals carry ancestral and spiritual significance. Birds such as the *ruru* (morepork owl) are often seen as *kaitiaki* (guardians) or signs from the spirit world. Animals such as whales, sharks, and lizards appear in creation stories and family lineages. After loss, many Māori look to nature for signs of spiritual presence, such as a bird call, a shadow, a visit from a guardian animal, offering comfort that the *wairua* (spirit) endures.

✲ Sami (Northern Scandinavia)

In Sami tradition, animals are not just companions but mediators between humans and the unseen world. The reindeer, central to Sami life, represents both survival and spiritual guidance. Shamans, or *noaidi*, call on animal spirits for healing and to navigate the unseen world, reflecting a deep, reciprocal relationship with nature.

✳ Chinese Traditional Beliefs

Chinese cosmology assigns animals powerful roles in maintaining harmony and balance. The dragon represents vitality and divine energy, the phoenix symbolises renewal and grace, and the tortoise embodies endurance and longevity. While the zodiac connects people to animal archetypes through birth years, traditional beliefs also link certain animals to mourning, honouring the dead, and maintaining ancestral relationships through rituals and offerings.

✳ Inuit (Arctic Regions)

Among Inuit communities, animals are not only vital to physical survival but also carry spiritual importance. For example, whales, seals, and polar bears are both vital for survival and spiritually revered. Whales bring abundance, seals are honoured for their gifts, and polar bears embody strength and intelligence. Hunters and shamans may communicate with animal spirits for guidance, healing, or understanding life transitions. Respectful rituals accompany hunting to maintain balance with the natural world. Grief is experienced within this spiritual ecology, connecting humans, animals, and the wider environment.

✳ Aztec & Mayan Traditions

In Aztec and Mayan belief systems, each person was born under the influence of a *tonal* (or *nahualli*), a spirit animal companion linked to their destiny based on their birth date. While Nahuals were important in Aztec cultures, the Mayan's focused on spiritual power of the individual, also referred to as Way. These animals were thought to protect, guide, and reflect aspects of one's soul. Jaguars, eagles, and snakes were especially sacred, embodying strength, power, sight, and rebirth. Animal spirits, such as dogs were central to rituals around death, ensuring that the soul transitioned safely and retained its connection to the living.

Animal Wisdom & Daily Practices

Number	Animal	Power	Core meaning	Page
1	Eagle	Spirit Above the Storm	Oneness	30
2	Hawk	The Messenger in the Silence	Messenger	34
3	Elk	The Guardian of Endless Paths	Stamina	38
4	Deer	The Keeper of Gentle Steps	Gentleness	42
5	Bear	The Watcher of the Hidden Heart	Introspection	46
6	Snake	The Weaver of Renewal	Transmutation	50
7	Skunk	The Keeper of Respect	Reputation	54
8	Otter	The Bringer of Joyful Waters	Play	58
9	Butterfly	The Herald of Metamorphosis	Transformation	62
10 / 1	Turtle	Mother Earth	Mother Earth	66
11	Moose	The Sentinel of Strength	Self-esteem	70
12 / 3	Porcupine	The Grace of Innocence	Innocence	74
13 / 4	Coyote	Wisdom and Folly	Joker	78
14 / 5	Dog	The Power of Loyalty	Loyalty	82
15 / 6	Wolf	The Pathfinder	Teacher	86
16 / 7	Raven	The Messenger of Hidden Truths	Magic	90
17 / 8	Mountain Lion	The Keeper of Courageous Vision	Leadership	94
18 / 9	Lynx	The Keeper of Secrets	Observation	98
19 / 1	Buffalo	Guardian of Gratitude and Abundance	Gratitude	102
20 / 2	Mouse	Keeper of Detail and Awareness	Scrutiny	106
21 / 3	Owl	Keeper of Silent Wisdom	Silent Wisdom	110
22	Beaver	The Master Builder	Industriousness	114
23 / 5	Opossum	The Art of Diversion	Diversion	118
24 / 6	Crow	The Law Keeper	Law	121
25 / 7	Fox	Master of Camouflage	Camouflage	125
26 / 8	Squirrel	Gathering with Purpose	Gathering	128
27 / 9	Dragonfly	Illusion and Perception	Illusion	132
28 / 1	Armadillo	Guarding Boundaries	Boundaries	136
29 / 11 / 2	Badger	Keeper of Stories	Stories	140

Number	Animal	Power	Core meaning	Page
30 / 3	Rabbit	Overcoming Fear	Fear	144
31 / 4	Turkey	The Gift of Sacrifice	Sacrifice	148
32 / 5	Ant	The Patience of Time	Patience	152
33	Weasel	Master of Stealth	Stealth	156
34 / 7	Grouse	The Sacred Spiral of Life	Doorway	160
35 / 8	Horse	The Power of Freedom	Power	163
36 / 9	Lizard	The Dreamer's Path	Perception	168
37 / 1	Antelope	The Speed of Action	Action	172
38 / 11 / 2	Frog	The Cleansing Song of Water and Sound	Cleansing	175
39 / 3	Swan	The Grace of Transformation	Grace	179
40 / 4	Dolphin	The Song of Breath and Sound	Breath	183
41 / 5	Whale	The Ancient Song of Creation	Creation	188
42 / 6	Bat	The Harbinger of Rebirth	Rebirth	193
43 / 7	Spider	The Weaver of Fate	Creative Power	197
44	Hummingbird	The Joy of Lightness	Wonder	201
45 / 9	Blue Heron	The Mirror of Self-Reflection	Self-Reflection	205
46 / 1	Raccoon	The Master of Dexterity and Disguise	Dexterity	209
47 / 11 / 2	Prairie Dog	The Wisdom of Retreat	Retreat	213
48 / 3	Wild Boar	The Courage of Confrontation	Confrontation	217
49 / 4	Salmon	The Wisdom of Inner Knowing	Wisdom	221
50 / 5	Alligator	The Power of Integration	Initiation and Integration	225
51 / 6	Jaguar	The Integrity of Impeccability	Integrity	229
52 / 7	Black Panther	Embracing the Mystery of the Unknown	Mystery	233
53 / 8	Lioness	The Power of Feminine Assertion	Feminine power	237
54 / 9	Elephant	The Ancient Power of Royalty	Royalty and strength	241
55	Bee	The Sweetness of Life's Nectar	Fertility	245
56 / 11 / 2	Tiger	The Power of Passion	Passion	249

1
Eagle

Oneness (1)

Spirit Above
the Storm

The eagle embodies the power of the number 1 — leadership and independence. It guides you to take control of your grief, seeing the bigger picture.

* **Opportunity:** To develop a higher perspective and leadership in your own healing process.
* **Grief Challenges:** Feeling lost or disconnected from one's identity; struggling to find a new path after loss. To overcome feelings of isolation and learn to soar above immediate grief.

Questions for today:
How can you rise above your grief today and view your emotions from a higher perspective? What daily habits lift your spirit? Have you been spending too much time alone, trying to maintain a form of independence? Have you been doubting yourself and needing to find more confidence in how you move forward?

Affirmations
- "I rise above challenges with clarity and vision."
- "I am strong and resilient, and am confident I can find a way forward."

Self-Care activities
Spend time in outside if you can. When outside, take a moment and observe the sky. This activity helps you connect with the Eagle's expansive spirit and gain a broader perspective on your journey. Collect feathers, or find photos of eagles, or watch a documentary about this great bird. Visit a mountaintop or a lookout and breathe in the fresh air while you see a vast horizon.

Story
Eagle embodies the qualities of vision, freedom, and spiritual connection across various cultures, seeing them rising high above the earth yet seeing with extraordinary clarity. Across cultures, it symbolises strength of spirit, the courage to soar beyond limitations, and the wisdom that comes from a higher perspective. Eagle reminds us that when we rise above immediate struggles, we can glimpse the wider pattern of our journey.

In Greek mythology, Eagle was sacred to Zeus, the King of the Gods, embodying divine authority and the power of the skies. In some Native

American traditions, the Eagle is honoured as a messenger between humans and the Creator, carrying prayers upward and returning with spiritual insight. While in ancient Egypt the falcon of Horus carried many of the qualities we now associate with Eagle, both birds represented vision, protection, and the guardianship of the soul.

Fable | Spirit Above the Storm
Long ago, when the earth was still young, the winds challenged all creatures to climb the highest peak. Many turned back when the air grew thin. Only Eagle rose above the clouds. The winds tried to break its wings, but Eagle spread them wider, letting the storm lift it higher. From that day, it was given the gift of sight beyond the horizon, to see what others could not.

The Eagle, majestic and proud, soared high above the jagged peaks where the sky kissed the earth. It lived above the world's chaos, nesting in the highest cliffs, where only the fiercest winds dared to blow. Its wings, vast and powerful, glided effortlessly through the thin mountain air, cutting through clouds like a blade of light. The Eagle saw all from its vantage, its piercing gaze illuminating both the bright and the shadowed places below.

Once, a young Falcon struggled up the mountainside, battered by the same wild winds. It faltered, ready to give in. Eagle swooped beside it and shared the currents of air beneath its wings. "Do not fight the wind," Eagle whispered, "rise with it." The Falcon steadied, lifted by the same storm that once threatened to break it.

With newfound courage, the Falcon spread its wings and launched itself into the wind, feeling the currents differently this time. The Eagle watched as the Falcon soared higher, understanding now that the key to the heights lay not in avoiding the shadows, but in embracing the balance of both.

This is the way of Spirit. Eagle does not flee storms. It rises through them.

It teaches that true strength is not in resisting pain, but trusting you can rise beyond it.

Eagle teaches that real courage is not only about facing life's storms but also about trusting in our ability to rise again. Its flight reminds us that grief and healing involve moments of descent and ascent, each offering wisdom, each strengthening our wings for the journey ahead.

2
Hawk

Messenger (2)

The Messenger
in the Silence

The hawk, aligned with the number 2, represents partnership and communication. It reminds you to stay open to signs from the Universe and your loved ones.

* **Opportunity:** To open yourself to intuitive guidance and messages from the Universe.

* **Grief Challenges:** Difficulty maintaining balance in relationships; feeling isolated or unsupported. To overcome confusion and stay receptive to signs and messages during grief. Being overly sensitive to others words or meanings.

Questions for today:
Are you listening to the messages that grief is sending you? How can you be more present and attentive to your inner voice? Are you feeling out of balance? Are you making too many compromises for others? Have you found you have lashed out with words and need to make amends? Are you considering other ways to make connections with your loved one? Find a way to balance your priorities. Consider where you are making compromises, (or need to), such as your work, relationships or health.

Affirmations
- "I listen to the messages from my heart."
- "I am open to receiving guidance and messages from the Universe."

Self-Care activities
Write a message to yourself. Create a note or letter where you offer kind words of encouragement and guidance. This act reflects the Hawk's role as a messenger and provides you with supportive reminders. Take care of your eyes; less screen time, soothing oils, weighted eye-pillow.

Story
Hawk is a vigilant presence, its sharp eyes scanning the horizon with unbroken focus. It is often remembered as a messenger, bridging the realms of the earthly and the divine, urging us to pay attention to the signs and subtleties that surround us. Hawk calls us to clarity and discernment, guiding us to trust our instincts and to see beyond appearances.

In Greco-Roman tradition, Hawk was linked with Apollo, god of prophecy, and Mercury, the swift messenger, strengthening its role as a bearer of insight and divine communication. Celtic lore viewed Hawk and other birds of prey as omens of clear-sightedness and guides into hidden truths, reminding people to read the unseen currents of life with care.

Hawk teaches us that healing requires awareness - the ability to watch for messages, to recognise guidance when it arrives, and to trust that clarity emerges when we look with both heart and spirit. Its flight reminds us to stay attentive, for wisdom often comes quietly, carried on the winds of our own perception.

Hawk lives between the seen and the unseen. It rides the thin currents of air just above the earth, watching with a steady eye. Hawk teaches that messages are everywhere, waiting to be recognised, in chance conversations, words overheard, sudden thoughts out of nowhere, in symbols in dreams, in the memory of someone you love.

Fable | The Messenger in the Silence
In grief, your world can shrink to what is directly in front of you. Every path seems blurred. You move through the days on instinct, unsure where to place your next step. It is in this silence that Hawk appears.

Long ago, when the forest was tangled with shadow, a young Deer stood frozen in the forest, unsure which way to turn. Its heart was full but heavy, every step uncertain. Hawk watched from above and saw a hidden trail curling through the trees. With a tilt of its wings, Hawk cast a fleeting shadow across the clearing. Deer lifted its head and followed where the shadow fell. The way forward revealed itself, not as a map, but as a feeling. The Hawk's message was clear: in times of confusion, trust the signs and messages that come from unexpected places. These are the whispers of the Universe, guiding you forward.

This is Hawk's gift. It teaches you to rise above the noise without leaving your heart behind, to rise just enough above your pain to see the wider shape of your life. Not to escape the grief, but to notice the quiet signals guiding you through it. To see the message within the moment. In grief, your senses may dull. Hawk calls them back to life. It reminds you to attune your senses, to pause, breathe and notice what is moving around you and within you. When you open to partnership with the world, you begin to see that you are not alone. Messages arrive in the smallest of ways. You are not lost. There are signs. The Universe has not stopped speaking. Let Hawk show you how to read the unseen language of your life.

3
Elk

Stamina (3)

The Guardian
of Endless Paths

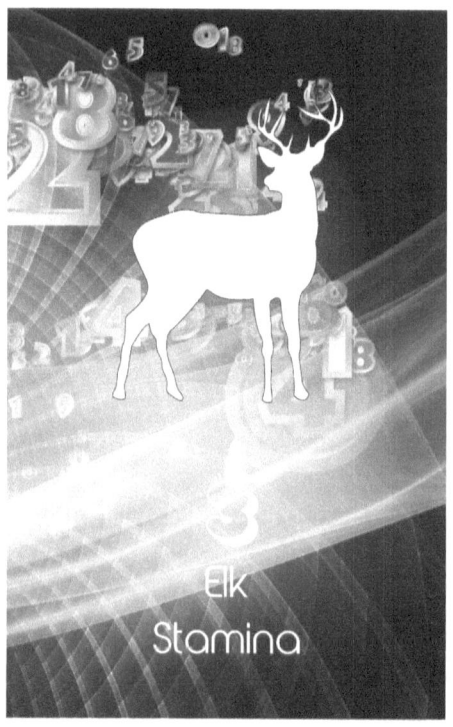

The elk's endurance resonates with the number 3, symbolising growth and creativity. It encourages you to keep creating ways to move forward, even when the path is difficult. It teaches you to pace yourself in your healing journey, knowing that persistence is key to overcoming grief.

- **Opportunity:** To build resilience and persist through emotional challenges.
- **Challenge:** To overcome feelings of weakness and maintain endurance through your grief.

Questions for today:
How are you nurturing your strength and stamina through this difficult time? What habits can you cultivate to help you sustain your energy? Have you been relying heavily on your friends and family to distract you from your grief? What creative pursuit have you neglected as a result of your grief that would help you during this time? Have you been viewing life as a glass half empty?

Affirmations
- "I have the stamina to endure and overcome any obstacle."
- "I embrace life with strength and endurance."
- "I have what it takes to continue my healing journey."

Self-Care Activities
Go for a brisk walk. Engage in a walk or light exercise that energises you and allows you to physically express yourself. This activity mirrors the Elk's stamina and helps build physical and mental resilience. Start a creative project you have put off for a while, or begin something special and unique that expresses who you are right now.

Story
In ancient teachings, Elk was revered as a creature of stamina and quiet strength, a living symbol of resilience and the capacity to endure life's trials with dignity. Among many Native American traditions, Elk is remembered for its steady presence and noble bearing, representing endurance that comes not from force, but from balance and harmony with the natural world. Its great antlers, renewed each year, were often seen as rising bridges between earth and spirit, a reminder of cycles of growth and the sacred link between the physical and the divine.

In Norse mythology, the great stags who browse upon the branches of Yggdrasil, the World Tree, carry echoes of Elk, embodying the untamed vitality of the forest and the constant renewal of nature. In Celtic tradition, the stag was associated with sovereignty and the mysteries of the Otherworld, guiding seekers across thresholds into deeper wisdom and spiritual truth.

Elk's way of moving through the world teaches patience and perseverance. Healing, like Elk's long journey, is not a race but a steady path taken step by step. By allowing ourselves to rest when needed, to rise when ready, and to keep moving forward with quiet determination, we honour the slow but certain growth that emerges through endurance, balance, and renewal.

Fable | The Guardian of Endless Paths

When grief stretches endlessly ahead, you may feel worn thin, as if you will never reach the far side of the season. This is when Elk comes.

Elk carries an ancient rhythm. It does not rush. It endures. Its antlers rise like living branches, renewing each year, proof that strength can return after every loss. Elk embodies creativity and expression, flowing in cycles of three - a reminder that inspiration often emerges in patterns, sequences, and rhythms, even when life feels heavy.

Once, an Otter darted alongside Elk at the forest's edge, splashing through streams and racing ahead with bursts of energy. But soon Otter grew tired, and the forest still stretched on. "Why do you move so slowly?" Otter asked, panting. Elk paused and breathed deeply. "I move with the land, not against it. My power is not in haste but in holding my ground, one step at a time. Finding a way forward requires creativity, and this comes not from rushing but from moving with awareness, letting ideas and expression emerge naturally."

Otter rested and watched as Elk moved forward, unhurried and unwavering. The path did not shorten, but it felt less impossible. The Elk's lesson became clear: true progress is made not through speed, but through perseverance and the creative ways we adapt to life's challenges.

This is Elk's gift. It reminds you that healing is not a sprint but a steady return of strength, step by step, even when the path ahead is unseen. Your creativity, like your resilience, unfolds in its own natural rhythm.

In grief, your energy arrives in fragments. Elk teaches you to gather it, pace your heart, and trust in the slow rebuilding of your spirit. You are still moving. You are still creating. Like Elk, you are far stronger than you realise.

4
Deer

Gentleness (4)

The Keeper of Gentle Steps

The deer, linked to the number 4, embodies stability and gentle strength. It teaches you to approach your grief with tenderness, creating a safe, grounded space for healing.

- **Opportunity:** To develop compassion and gentle self-care during your healing journey.
- **Challenge:** To overcome harsh self-judgement and cultivate a nurturing attitude towards yourself and others. To not be so rigid in your approach.

Questions for today:
Are you being gentle with yourself as you navigate grief? What daily act of kindness can you give to yourself today? What daily routines will help you move forward that you can start using today? Do you need to take a gentler approach with others around you, in order for you to also help them?

Affirmation:
- "I embrace gentleness and compassion towards myself and others."
- "I move through grief with gentle grace."

Self-Care Activities
Practice self-compassion. Take a moment to speak kindly to yourself, perhaps through affirmations or gentle self-talk. If you find this challenging, think how you would speak to yourself as a child, encouraging them and finding key words that open your heart. This practice reflects the Deer's gentle nature and builds a nurturing self-relationship.

Story
In ancient teachings, Deer was revered for its gentleness and quiet strength, moving softly through the forest yet alert to every sound. Among Native American traditions, Deer is remembered as a guide of peace and compassion, teaching that resilience can emerge through tenderness rather than force. Its soft gaze and graceful step embodied a harmony that offered safety to those who followed its path.

In Celtic mythology, Roe deer was linked with the goddess Flidais, a guardian of the forest and provider of abundance. Deer were also regarded as messengers of the Otherworld, leading seekers between realms and inviting them to walk in humility and grace. In Buddhist tradition, Deer are remembered for their presence at Sarnath, where the Buddha first taught, symbolising the sacred act of listening with an open heart.

Deer's way of being teaches us that healing often begins with compassion. By allowing softness and care to guide us through grief, we discover that vulnerability is not weakness but a pathway to strength and connection.

Artemis, the Goddess of the hunt, is often depicted with deer, symbolising protection during childbirth and the care of children. Her teachings emphasise the importance of caring for oneself and others during the healing process.

In the wild, a deer moves with quiet awareness, sensing the rhythms of its environment and responding with care. Every step is deliberate, reflecting a natural balance between caution and curiosity. Its behaviour demonstrates responsibility and dedication, emerging from the need to live in harmony with its surroundings. The deer's attentiveness to its environment shows how strength can be grounded in observation, patience, and gentle persistence rather than force.

Fable | The Keeper of Gentle Steps
When grief or pressure weighs heavily on you, it can feel as if the ground beneath your feet is unsteady. Deer comes to guide you.

A Badger once paused while burrowing, frustrated by obstacles in its path. "Why are you so gentle and quiet?" it asked Deer. "Life is hard. Sometimes you must fight to survive."

Deer lifted its head, ears attuned to the wind. "Strength is not always loud," it said. "I move with care, listening and observing. Stability comes from understanding the land, respecting its rhythms, and responding with intention. Structure does not bind me. It supports me."

The Badger looked doubtful. "But what about when danger comes?"

"Even then," Deer replied, "my gentleness allows me to sense shifts in the environment. I notice patterns others miss. I act with responsibility, maintaining boundaries and rules that keep my world secure. True power lies in consistency and presence, not always aggression."

The Deer's soft, yet stable approach offered a new way to navigate life: not through constant defence, but by allowing room for gentleness and self-compassion.

By following natural paths and attuning itself to the subtle cues of the forest, the deer embodies grounding and stability. Its presence reminds us that structure and routine are not limitations, but guides that help us navigate life with grace. Through its quiet vigilance, Deer teaches that resilience is nurtured when we move thoughtfully, honour natural rhythms, and respond to the world with both sensitivity and intention.

Ultimately, Deer invites us to embrace healing and growth as processes that unfold gently, showing that true strength is cultivated in harmony with the wisdom of nature.

5
Bear

Introspection (5)
The Watcher of the Hidden Heart

Bear, with the energy of the number 5, represents introspection and change. It guides you to have the discipline to retreat within yourself to process your grief and emerge stronger, seeking freedom from the daily struggles of life.

* **Opportunity:** To engage in self-reflection and gain deeper insights into your healing process.
* **Challenge:** To overcome distractions and take meaningful time for introspection and self-discovery.

Questions for today:
Have you allowed yourself the space to reflect on your grief? What quiet time can you carve out each day to connect with your deeper feelings? What new avenues of change can help you consider finding relief from your grief? Have you been too excessive with your isolation and need to re-enter the world? Have you had an apathetic mindset to people or activities that requires review? Are you not wanting to face the changes now present in your reality?

Affirmation:
- "I take time for introspection and self-discovery."
- "I find freedom in solitude."

Self-Care Activities
Engage in reflective journaling. Set aside time to write down your thoughts and feelings. Create a mind map to see where your emotions are focused. This introspective activity aligns with the Bear's focus on deep self-reflection and inner exploration. Start a new routine focused on helping yourself in your grief journey and start small to help you be consistent and disciplined. In your discipline you will feel freedom.

Story
In ancient teachings, Bear was honoured as a creature of immense strength and deep introspection, a guardian of both courage and healing. For many Native American peoples, Bear was a symbol of protection and medicine, guiding those who sought inner power through solitude and self-reflection. Its ability to retreat into the earth during winter and emerge renewed became a sacred reminder of life's cycles of rest and rebirth.

In Norse tradition, warriors known as berserkers were said to take on the spirit of the bear, embodying its ferocity in battle. In Celtic mythology, the goddess Artio was associated with Bear, revered as a guardian of fertility, abundance, and protection. Ursa Major and Ursa Minor (Greek Mythology), are constellations linked to the story of Callisto, transformed into a bear. This connection highlights themes of transformation, protection, and the nurturing aspects of bears. The bear is often associated with maternal instincts and protection. This symbolises the importance of nurturing relationships and creating a safe space for healing.

Bear's way of living teaches that healing requires rhythm, a time for strength and a time for rest. By honouring the dark seasons of retreat as much as the bright seasons of action, we learn to trust the cycles that restore us, emerging with renewed courage and wisdom. The Bear teaches that in grief, it is necessary to find quiet moments to reflect and process, allowing transformation to happen naturally from within.

Bear embodies introspection, discipline, and the courage to embrace change. Its retreats into solitude are not avoidance, they are purposeful pauses to understand your inner world. Bear reminds you that reflection is a form of strength. Freedom emerges when you know yourself, and transformation requires disciplined observation of your thoughts, emotions, actions and patterns.

Fable | The Watcher of the Hidden Heart
When life feels heavy, grief can cloud your clarity. Bear comes to guide you.

One Winter, Bear wandered through the quiet forest, preparing for hibernation. The leaves fell, the air chilled, and the forest slowed. A young Wolf, eager but restless, observed Bear's deliberate movements and asked,

"Why do you retreat into the mountains when the world is busy? There is so much to do, so many demands."

Bear looked down, calm and steady. "I retreat to see clearly," it said. "The forest moves fast, and it is easy to get lost in the noise. By pausing, by looking inward, I understand what matters. I do not shut out the world. I gain freedom and strength to move with purpose when the time comes."

The Wolf tilted its head, uncertain. "What if I miss opportunities by resting?"

Bear's deep voice rumbled with wisdom. "Opportunities come to those who know themselves. Change is constant. By observing and reflecting, I navigate the shifts in my life and the world around me. Discipline in introspection allows me to emerge stronger, prepared, and free to act intentionally rather than reactively." The Bear's journey into the mountains was not one of escape, but of transformation.

Bear teaches you that grief and self-reflection can coexist. Its solitude is a sanctuary for understanding your needs and your power. In discipline, Bear finds freedom. In reflection, Bear finds clarity. In embracing change, Bear models how to navigate life with patience, awareness, and resilience.

6
Snake

Transmutation (6)
The Weaver
of Renewal

Snake, aligned with the number 6, represents transformation, transmutation and balance. It teaches you to let go of old grief, allowing for renewal and healing through a nurturing practice.

* **Opportunity:** To embrace transformation and allow yourself to heal and grow.
* **Challenge:** To overcome resistance to change and accept the process of personal renewal.

Questions for today
How can you transform the pain of grief into something healing today? What small daily change could shift your perspective? What old parts of you are keeping you stuck in your grief? How are feelings of victimisation holding you back? What habit do you need to break to help you move forward? How can you provide nurturing support to others?

Affirmation:
- "I embrace transformation and the healing process."
- "I allow change and shed the old to welcome the new."

Self-Care Activities
Take a cleansing bath with a good loofah! Participate in a ritual that symbolises renewal and transformation. This practice helps embrace the Snake's ability to shed old layers and transform. Do a grounding exercise with somatic therapy ideas. Clear a cluttered bench or space you've been meaning to get to. Delete old emails and photos that you no longer need as you move forward. Print photos and frame them, highlighting people you love and moments you cherish.

Story
In ancient teachings, Snake was revered as a symbol of transformation, shedding its skin to reveal renewal and new life. Among many Indigenous traditions, Snake carried the wisdom of cycles, death, and rebirth, embodying the mysteries of healing and regeneration. Its movement close to the earth linked it to grounding, fertility, and the hidden energies of nature. The shedding of its skin is a potent metaphor for letting go of the old, allowing for personal transmutation and healing.

In Greek mythology, the serpent entwined around the rod of Asclepius became a lasting emblem of medicine and healing and is still used today for logos and symbols in modern medicine. In Hindu tradition, the coiled serpent known as Kundalini represented the latent spiritual energy waiting to awaken and rise through the body.

In Norse mythology, Jörmungandr, the Midgard Serpent, represents the cyclical nature of life, destruction and renewal. This connection highlights the importance of recognising the interconnectedness of all beings. The feathered serpent God Quetzalcoatl in Mesoamerican Mythology represents the duality of life and death, symbolising the cycle of transformation and renewal. His teachings emphasise the importance of embracing change and understanding the cycles of life.

Snake's way of shedding reminds us that healing often demands release. By letting go of what no longer serves us, we step into renewal, carrying forward only what is essential for growth.

Snake embodies transformation and renewal, guiding you to release what no longer serves you and create space for growth. It also represents harmony and nurturing, showing you how to balance inner healing with care for yourself and others.

In your grief journey, Snake whispers that letting go is not just about shedding the past - it is about cultivating inner harmony. Old patterns, thoughts, sorrow, and limiting beliefs can weigh you down. Snake teaches that healing requires both release and gentle self-nurture.

Fable | The Weaver of Renewal
A young Fox watched Snake shed its skin, smooth and renewed. "How do you do that?" the Fox asked. "How do you let go and remain whole?".

"I do not resist the process of change," the Snake replied. "I understand that growth requires shedding what no longer serves me. To hold on to my old skin would only keep me trapped in what I used to be."

Snake's eyes met the Fox's, steady and calm. "Change can feel uncomfortable," it said. "But clinging to the old only disrupts my harmony. By shedding my old skin, I make room for new growth. The past may feel safe, but it can also become a burden, keeping me stuck in old grief and feeling like a victim."

The Fox hesitated. "What if I'm not ready?"

Snake slithered closer, voice soft yet firm. "Readiness comes in time. Transmutation requires patience. With each layer you shed, your spirit becomes lighter. As you release, allow yourself care and compassion. Healing is both letting go and nurturing what remains. The inner you has grown and you have no reason to keep showing the world the older, smaller version of yourself."

Snake teaches that true harmony comes from embracing transformation while tending to your inner self. Grief can coexist with nurturing and peace, and each step forward is a renewal of strength, clarity, hope and life.

7
Skunk

Reputation (7)
The Keeper
of Respect

Skunk's connection to the number 7 symbolises introspection and reputation. It encourages you to honour your grief journey without worrying about others' perceptions.

- **Opportunity:** To reinforce your personal values and integrity during your healing journey.
- **Challenge:** To overcome doubts about your reputation and remain steadfast in your principles.

Questions for today:
How has grief affected your sense of self-worth or how you present yourself? What habits could help restore your self-esteem? Whose opinion are you most worried about and why? Have you become disconnected with others and your larger purpose in life? Are you more focused on your reputation than your character and values?

Affirmations:
- "I honour my reputation and remain true to my values."
- "I protect my boundaries with dignity and grace."

Self-Care activities
Evaluate your values. Reflect on the qualities you want to be known for and ensure your actions align with these values. Consider both your *means* values and *ends* values in this practice. This activity helps reinforce your reputation and personal integrity. Take time to research more about yourself and how you communicate, act and think.

Story
In ancient teachings, Skunk was recognised for its unique power, a small creature with the ability to command respect without aggression. Among Native American traditions, Skunk was regarded as a teacher of reputation and boundaries, reminding people that the way they carried themselves determined the way others responded. Its striking markings and unmistakable presence were reminders that strength can come from quiet confidence.

Embracing who we are, even in moments of vulnerability, can empower us to restore our sense of self-worth and connection to the world. Skunks exude confidence through their unique defence mechanism. Their presence encourages individuals to embrace their self-worth and stand firm in their identities, especially during difficult times. Skunks are known for their ability to defend themselves with their spray, symbolising the importance of setting boundaries.

Their teachings encourage individuals to protect their emotional well-being during the grieving process. They are unapologetically themselves, representing the importance of authenticity. Skunk's way of being teaches us that healing requires boundaries. By standing firm in our truth and walking with dignity, we create spaces of safety where renewal can take place. Respect, once claimed, need not be fought for — it flows naturally from self-assurance and integrity.

In modern western culture, the famous cartoon character of Pepe Le Pew's entire persona revolves around how others perceive him, his overpowering scent precedes him, shaping his reputation before he even speaks. This mirrors the Skunk's symbolic link to reputation and self-assured presence, showing that how one carries themselves can command respect, or resistance, based on the impression they leave.

Fable | The Keeper of Respect
Skunk moves slowly through the forest, sensing the currents of the unseen. It stops to observe patterns, listen to the whispers of the world, and contemplate the meaning behind events. In doing so, it analyses not just the environment but the self.

A young Crow, anxious and impatient, called out: "Skunk, how do you move with such confidence when the world judges you?"

Skunk raised its head, calm and unwavering. "My scent, my appearance, and my choices may invite misunderstanding," it said. "Yet I honour my path, my integrity, and my values. Reputation is a reflection of action, not fear. I know that I must honour my grief without being weighed down by others' views. I can choose to embrace my journey, knowing that it contributes to my character and reputation.

To grieve fully and to act with self-respect, is to build true authority within myself."

The Crow hesitated. "But what if others reject me?"

Skunk's eyes glimmered with awareness. "Rejection is not a measure of worth. Understanding your inner truth and nurturing your spirit allows you to navigate both the physical and metaphysical world. Stand firm, act from integrity, and the unseen forces will guide you." Skunk teaches that in times of uncertainty, embracing introspection, study, and awareness of hidden patterns allows you to protect your self-respect, honour your grief, and step into the unseen currents of life with confidence.

Reputation is often shaped by perceptions, but your true essence cannot be diminished by the opinions of others. Your journey through grief is yours alone, and it deserves to be honoured. Focus on nurturing your values and integrity. When you stand firm in who you are, the world will come to recognise your strength, regardless of preconceived notions. Skunk's lesson is clear: Grief and self-respect coexist. By honouring your inner wisdom, you protect your reputation, cultivate discernment, and emerge aligned with both the visible and unseen realms.

8
Otter

Play (8)
The Bringer
of Joyful Waters

The Otter, resonating with the number 8, represents abundance and generosity. It reminds you to seek and give joy and support within your community during your grief. This is powerfully aligned with feminine energy, so now is a time to honour the support of the Sisterhood.

* **Opportunity:** To nurture yourself and find joy even in the midst of grief.
* **Challenge:** To overcome neglect of self-care and embrace the joy and comfort available to you.

Questions for today
Are you allowing space for joy and play amidst your grief? What playful activity could bring lightness into your day? Where is your Sisterhood at today – how about arrange a catch up? How do you connect with them, in person, online, by phone? How are you empowering yourself to move forward? What long term view do you have of where you want to be in the future? Have you focused too much on being responsible and working hard, rather than enjoying the moments that come with laughter and play?

Affirmation:
- "I embrace the nurturing and healing qualities within me."
- "I nurture myself and others with love and compassion."

Self-Care Activities
Enjoy a playful or empowering activity. Engage in something fun and light-hearted, catch up with girlfriends or find time to connect with feminine energy. This practice reflects the Otter's joyful spirit and contributes to emotional healing through playfulness.

Story
In ancient teachings, Otter was remembered for its joy and playfulness, a creature who brought lightness to heavy moments. Among Native American traditions, Otter embodied curiosity and feminine energy, teaching the wisdom of laughter, trust, community and the 'sisterhood'. Its ease in both water and land reflects adaptability and harmony with life's shifting currents and allowing emotions to flow while remaining grounded.

In Celtic lore, Otter was seen as a loyal companion to heroes, guiding them across rivers and offering help when least expected and was often called a 'water dog'. It symbolised friendship, resourcefulness, and the gift of delight even in times of uncertainty.

During times of grief, the Otter teaches us to embrace both our emotions, allowing ourselves to find joy while honouring our feelings of loss. By leaning into the support of our sisterhood and community, we can navigate through grief with greater ease, finding moments of abundance and connection even in our darkest times.

Otter's way of living teaches that healing need not always be solemn. By making space for joy, creativity, and play, we rediscover the simple moments that restore the heart and remind us of the goodness still present in life.

Fable | The Bringer of Joyful Waters
The Otter, playful and full of life, glided effortlessly through the sparkling waters of the river, its energy bright and unrestrained. It noticed a Turtle drifting alone, shoulders heavy with unseen burdens.

The Otter called out cheerfully, "Hey there, Turtle! Why do you seem so heavy today?"

The Turtle sighed, "I've been feeling lost since my friend left this world. The water doesn't feel the same anymore, and I can't seem to find joy in anything."

The Otter swam closer, its playful nature radiating warmth. "I understand that grief can feel like a stormy sea, but remember, you don't have to navigate it alone. Look around you, our community is here to support you. Together, we can find moments of joy amidst the sadness."

The Turtle hesitated. "But how can I feel joy when I miss my friend so much?"

With a gentle smile, the Otter replied, "Joy and grief can coexist. You do not need to choose one over the other. It's okay to cherish the memories while still allowing happiness into your heart. Have you thought about reaching out to our friends? Reach out. Connect. Celebrate the memories, share laughter, and allow love to flow into your heart. Strength grows in connection, and abundance is not only in what we have but in how we share it."

The Turtle pondered this, looking at the shimmering water reflecting the sunlight. "I suppose I've been hiding away, thinking I needed to grieve in silence and have felt guilty for feeling happy at small things."

The Otter nodded, understanding the importance of community in the healing journey. "Embrace the abundance of love and support around you. We are stronger together, and there is power in the connection we share. Allow yourself to play, to celebrate the moments of light that can lift your spirits, even if just for a while."

Linked with both water – emotion, and land – being grounded, allows you to find the flow in both worlds. To allow all emotions to flow, including those that are lighter and more joyful, and that by doing so, you too, like Otter, will likely be helping others in the process. It's ok to laugh, to smile if you catch yourself doing so.

9
Butterfly

Transformation (9)
The Herald
of Metamorphosis

Butterfly, linked to the number 9, signifies completion and transformation. It guides you to trust in the process of change and renewal in your grief, honouring the personal stages you will experience.

* **Opportunity:** To embrace your personal growth and transformation through the grieving process.
* **Challenge:** To overcome resistance to change and allow yourself to evolve through your grief.

Questions for today

What part of your grief journey is transforming you the most? How can you embrace change in your daily habits to support your healing? How can you tap into compassion to move you forward? What positive changes have you not given yourself credit for as part of your own growth journey? Do you need to forgive yourself? Are you acting like a martyr and not realising that your growth doesn't need to come from reciprocity or affirmation?

Affirmation:

- "I embrace the beauty of transformation and renewal."
- "I am growing and transforming through my grief."

Self-Care activities

Create a vision board. Assemble images and words that represent your future aspirations and goals. This activity symbolises the Butterfly's transformative journey and helps visualise personal growth and change. Think about what you can let go of, what is no longer serving you as you move toward a new identity.

Story

With wisdom passed down through ancient teachings, the Butterfly symbolises the journey of completion and renewal. It reminds us that transformation often follows grief, urging us to trust in the process of change and embrace our personal growth. The Butterfly teaches us to honour our experiences, knowing that transitioning through our grief is essential in shaping who we are becoming. By tapping into compassion for ourselves and others, we can navigate through our grief with grace, allowing our souls to evolve and find light even in the darkest times.

The Butterfly's metamorphosis from caterpillar to butterfly symbolises profound transformation. It teaches individuals to embrace change and the natural cycles of life, particularly in the grief process and see that there can be new beginnings, with growth through the pain of loss. Butterflies remind us that even difficult transitions can lead us to a different path. As creatures that flutter freely, butterflies symbolise lightness and joy. Their teachings encourage individuals to release the heaviness of grief and invite beauty back into their lives.

In Greek mythology, the Goddess Psyche, whose name means "Soul," is often depicted with butterfly wings. The metamorphosis of the butterfly inspired many to use butterflies as a symbol of the soul's exit from the body. In Aztec culture, Butterflies were seen as the spirits of warriors who had died in battle. They symbolised the soul's journey and the transition from the earthly world to the spiritual realm. In many Native American tribes, the Butterfly symbolises change, joy, hope and colour. It is believed that butterflies carry messages to the spirit world, signifying a connection between the living and the dead. In Japanese culture, Butterfly was a symbol of joy, grace, and the presence of departed loved ones.

Fable | The Herald of Metamorphosis
The Butterfly, a radiant symbol of transformation, fluttered gracefully among the blooming flowers of the meadow. One day, as it danced through the air, it noticed a Caterpillar resting on a leaf, looking despondent. The Caterpillar sighed heavily, its body weighed down by its own thoughts.

"Why do you seem so downcast?" asked the Butterfly, landing softly beside it. "You have the potential to become something magnificent."

The Caterpillar looked up, bewildered. "I'm afraid of change. The thought of becoming something entirely different terrifies me. I'm comfortable being this way."

The Butterfly gently flapped its wings, scattering a few petals into the breeze. "I understand your fear. I was once a Caterpillar too, bound to the earth and unsure of my future. But I learned that transformation is a natural part of life. Embracing change can lead to extraordinary possibilities."

The Caterpillar hesitated. "But what if I don't know who I'll be after I transform?"

The Butterfly flapped its wings softly, letting a breeze stir the petals around them. "I understand. I too was once grounded, unsure of what lay ahead. Change can feel frightening, but it is the path to growth and completion. Transformation does not erase who you are, it allows you to step fully into your potential."

"Every stage matters," the Butterfly said. "Even uncertainty and struggle carry lessons. Compassion for yourself is part of the journey. Forgive yourself for you doubt and hesitation. Each moment prepares you to emerge stronger and more whole."

The Caterpillar looked around at the vibrant meadow. The fear lingered, but a spark of hope had appeared. "Perhaps it is time to let go and trust the process," it whispered. The Butterfly lifted into the air. "Transformation begins when you embrace both fear and courage. Completion comes not in perfection, but in willingness to evolve and move forward with an open heart."

Butterfly's way of becoming teaches us that grief itself is a metamorphosis. In surrendering to change, we emerge transformed, carrying wings of resilience that remind us life can hold beauty after loss.

10
Turtle

Mother Earth (1)
Mother Earth

Turtle's connection to the number 10 represents wholeness and completion, ready for new beginnings with ancient authenticity and independence. It teaches you to take your time in healing, staying grounded in the support of nature and allowing your emotions to flow and not become stagnant.

* **Opportunity:** To find stability and grounding through connection with Mother Earth, including the ocean.
* **Challenge:** To overcome feelings of instability and cultivate a sense of grounding and security and being able to manage the ebb and flow of strong emotions.

Questions for today
Are you grounded in your grief, or do you feel unmoored? How can connecting with nature help ground you each day? What new path have you thought to take to help you with your grief that might be unconventional? How could you connect with the Season and focus more on nature? Have you tried to 'fake it until you make it' and felt lost in the lack of sincerity? Have you come to rely too much on others to help your mood or manage your own life rhythms? Have you lost your determination to move forward? Are you too determined to 'manage' your grief and 'get over' things?

Affirmation:
- "I connect with the nurturing energy of Mother Earth and find stability."
- "I move steadily forward, grounded in the wisdom of the Earth."

Self-Care activities
Connect with the earth or water in a new way! Spend time gardening or simply walking barefoot on natural ground, or having a relaxing bath or invigorating swim. This grounding activity reflects the Turtle's connection to Mother Earth and builds a sense of stability and connection. Immerse yourself in water. Plant a tree or plant in memory of your loved one and as a symbol of moving forward. Find time alone to reflect on your own independent journey.

Story
In ancient teachings, Turtle was revered as a creature of grounding and patience, carrying its home upon its back and moving with quiet determination. Among Native American traditions, Turtle was honoured as a symbol of Mother Earth herself, a being of creation,

endurance, and protection. Its slow, deliberate steps reflected the sacred rhythm of time and the wisdom of longevity. With their protective shells, turtles represent the importance of self-protection and grounding.

In Hindu mythology, the cosmic turtle Kurma bore the weight of the world, supporting creation through stability and strength. It is seen as a symbol of wisdom and the cycle of life and death.

Turtle's way of travelling teaches us that healing cannot be rushed. Each step, though small, carries us closer to wholeness. By grounding ourselves in patience and trusting the long journey, we discover the quiet strength that endures through time. In Aboriginal Australian culture, turtles hold deep significance, often representing creation, wisdom, and the interconnectedness of life. Many Dreamtime stories (the Aboriginal understanding of the world's origins) highlight the role of turtles in creation myths, embodying themes of perseverance, survival, and protection

In Hawaiian culture, the *honu* (turtle), is a revered symbol representing longevity, peace, and a connection between humans and the ocean. Turtles hold a sacred place in Hawaiian mythology and are seen as protectors of the land and guides in both the physical and spiritual realms. Their teachings remind individuals to approach grief and healing with patience, understanding that recovery may be a long journey.

Fable | Mother Earth
The Turtle, an ancient symbol of Mother Earth, its shell catching sunlight like a shield of wisdom. The Turtle glided through the deep blue ocean, each stroke deliberate and steady. Its shell shimmered under the sunlit waves, a testament to its journey through currents

and tides. Unlike the swirling waters around it, the Turtle moved at its own pace, guided by an inner compass.

A curious Dolphin swam alongside, leaping energetically. "Why do you move so calmly? The currents are strong and the reef is full of life. Don't you want to play with all of us?"

The Turtle drifted alongside, unwavering. "I follow my own path," it said. "The ocean is vast and full of possibilities, but I trust the rhythm that guides me. I do not need to rush or mimic others to know I am moving rightly."

The Dolphin paused, considering the words. "But what if the currents change or danger approaches?"

The Turtle dipped beneath a wave, glancing upward. "I remain grounded in who I am, aware of the waters but not ruled by them. Confidence comes from trusting my journey. My authenticity is shown in how I move with purpose, and my strength is staying true to myself. When I feel overwhelmed, I retreat into my shell, whether on land or beneath the water's surface, finding comfort in my connection to Mother Earth. It reminds me that I am supported and can face new beginnings." With that, the Turtle continued through the open water, each stroke a quiet assertion of its own power and path, showing that the ocean's expanse is best navigated when you trust yourself first.

11
Moose

Self-Esteem (11)

The Sentinel
of Strength

Moose, aligned with the master number 11, represents spiritual insight and self-esteem. It encourages you to recognise your inner strength and self-worth as you navigate grief.

* **Opportunity:** Moose offers the opportunity to rebuild self-worth and recognise one's intrinsic value, even when grief leaves you feeling lost.

* **Challenge:** The challenge is to overcome self-doubt and feelings of unworthiness, which often arise during grief.

Questions for today

How is grief challenging your sense of self-worth? What positive affirmation can you repeat daily to rebuild your self-esteem? What part of your sub-conscious are you ignoring? What other practices in other cultures could assist you in your healing journey? What wonderful affirmations from other people are you dismissing or forgetting?

Affirmation:

- "I honour my worth and embrace my personal power."
- "I stand tall in my truth and connect with something beyond myself."

Self-Care activities

Write a list of your strengths and achievements. Spend some time reflecting on your accomplishments and qualities that make you proud. This exercise can help boost self-esteem and remind you of your personal value. Research other cultures and their practices that support their grieving process. Spend time in front of the mirror and start practicing saying 'I love you'. It may feel uncomfortable at first, but it allows your Spirit to speak directly to you. Become aware of all your statements that begin with 'I am, I'm...'' and see what follows. If it is not supportive or kind, then perhaps it is time to re-evaluate those words and their impact.

Story

In ancient teachings, Moose was revered for its towering strength and quiet presence, a creature that moves through the wild with dignity and calm assurance. Among many Native American cultures, Moose represents self-esteem, guiding individuals to recognise their intrinsic worth and trust in their own abilities. Its great antlers, reaching skyward, symbolise the connection between earth and spirit, a reminder that confidence grows when we honour both our physical and spiritual selves.

Moose's solitary nature teaches that time alone is not loneliness but a sacred opportunity for reflection and inner growth. Its sure-footed movements through forests and marshes remind us to move deliberately, trusting our own path and pace.

The presence of Moose inspires us to navigate life's challenges with quiet confidence. Healing, like Moose's steady journey, requires patience, courage, and trust in one's own strength. By following Moose's example, we learn to stand tall, embrace our self-worth, and move forward with dignity even when the journey feels heavy.

Fable | The Sentinel of Strength
The Moose, towering and serene, stood in the quiet hush of the forest, its breath curling like mist in the morning light. Its antlers rose like living trees, ancient and wise, holding the weight of countless seasons. As it stepped through the stillness toward a glimmering stream, it paused, sensing the ache of Raven's sorrow.

"I know the heaviness you carry," said the Moose, its presence steady and unshaken. "Grief can make the ground feel unsteady, as though the world has forgotten your place within it. But strength is not something you must chase. It lives in you already, waiting to be remembered."

Raven watches as the Moose lowers its great head to drink, each movement slow and deliberate. "When doubt creeps in," it continues, "I return to the land that shaped me. I walk among the trees and let their stillness remind me of my own. I listen to the water and hear how it continues, even when the path bends unseen. Nature reflects back the truth I sometimes forget: I am worthy, I am still becoming."

The forest holds its breath as the Moose lifts its gaze to meet Raven. "You, too, can walk through this grief with dignity. Speak gently to yourself. Honour the strength that has carried you this far. Your pain is not a measure of your weakness, but of your love. Stand tall, even if your heart trembles. In time, your Spirit will remember how powerful it truly is."

Moose's presence, carrying the energy of spiritual awakening and higher vision reminds us that grief can be a threshold, calling you to rise beyond the physical and trust in the unseen. Like the antlers reaching towards the sky, Moose asks you to align with your inner wisdom, to see not only what has been lost but what sacred truth is being revealed. Through the Moose, you are reminded that even in sorrow, you are being guided toward your soul's higher path.

And then the Moose moves on, each step quiet yet certain, leaving behind the deep imprint of its path, reminder that you, too, can rise and continue, strong and steadfast, rooted in your own worth.

12
Porcupine

Innocence (3)

The Grace
of Innocence

Porcupine's connection to the number 12 represents the balance between innocence and protection. It encourages you to maintain a sense of wonder while setting healthy boundaries in your grief and to balance your pessimism with your optimism.

* **Opportunity:** Porcupine brings the gift of rediscovering your sense of wonder and play, helping you heal through reconnecting with simple joys.

* **Challenge:** The challenge is releasing cynicism and bitterness that may build up as a defence mechanism in grief, or feelings overly

pessimistic that you will never experience happiness again and that life has no joy.

Questions for today
Are you holding onto cynicism or bitterness in your grief? How can you reconnect with simple joys today? What ways can you embrace opening yourself up to love and joy again? What past hurts are stopping you from expressing happiness? Who can you allow yourself to be more vulnerable with? Are you being overly pessimistic about life, or overly optimistic – what are you missing? How can you express yourself in new ways that help you move forward?

Affirmation:
- "I embrace my innocence and find peace in simplicity."
- "I protect my heart while living life with childlike wonder."

Self-Care Activity
Create a comforting ritual. Light a candle and spend a few minutes enjoying a peaceful activity like reading a favourite book or listening to calming music. This helps in reconnecting with a sense of innocence and peace. Watch children playing, see the joy sparked by innocence in their learning and fun. Try opening up to a friend or coach, counsellor and see what it feels like to be more vulnerable.

Story
In ancient teachings, Porcupine was revered as a creature of gentle curiosity and quiet resilience. Among many Native American cultures, Porcupine represents innocence and protection, teaching that strength does not require aggression, and that boundaries can coexist with openness and trust. Its quills, sharp yet naturally shed, serve as

reminders that we can defend ourselves while moving through the world with care and playfulness.

Porcupine's presence encourages reflection and self-awareness, showing that even after hardship, it is possible to maintain a sense of wonder and a trusting approach to life. In some African folklore, Porcupine is celebrated as a clever and resourceful creature, demonstrating that intelligence and adaptability are forms of protection as powerful as physical strength.

Porcupine's way of living teaches that healing is a balance between safeguarding ourselves and remaining open to life's joys with an innocence of seeing in a new way. By respecting our own boundaries and allowing space for curiosity and play, we learn to navigate grief with resilience, gradually opening ourselves to love, joy, and renewed connection with the world around us.

Fable | The Grace of Innocence

The Porcupine, a gentle creature adorned with protective quills, wandered through a sunlit meadow where wildflowers danced in the breeze. Despite its spiky exterior, the Porcupine radiated an air of innocence and curiosity. One afternoon, it noticed a solemn Hedgehog curled tightly in the grass, as though the world had grown too sharp to face.

"Why do you stay hidden?" the Porcupine asked gently, stopping a safe distance away.

The Hedgehog lifted its head, eyes tired. "Grief has made everything feel dangerous. I've stopped reaching for anything that might hurt."

The Porcupine lowered itself into the grass so its voice would carry like a secret between them. "I understand that fear. My quills are my armour, but they do not stop me from seeking wonder. I still watch the clouds drift, still taste the sweetness of berries, still let the breeze kiss my nose. Protection does not mean closing the door on joy."

The Hedgehog uncurled slightly, uncertain. "But what if opening up brings more pain?"

"Then you let your quills do their work," the Porcupine said with a small smile. "You do not need to give up your boundaries to welcome life. You can be both cautious and curious. Wonder is not the absence of pain, but the choice to keep your heart open enough to notice beauty despite it."

A hush fell over the meadow. The Hedgehog slowly stood, the weight of sorrow easing just enough for a breath of hope to slip through.

"Vulnerability is not weakness," the Porcupine said. "It is the doorway to creation. When I let my soft heart be seen, ideas flow and life begins to feel bright again. We are not meant to live only behind our armour."

As the Porcupine moved on, it paused beside a patch of wildflowers blooming in a tumble of colour. It had learned that healing rarely comes in straight lines. Instead, it arrives like these blossoms, unexpected, untamed, and full of possibility for a brighter day. Grief had once made the Porcupine curl tightly into itself, quills bristling against the world. But over time, it discovered that creation itself could be a balm. When it allowed its heart to open, songs and colours and small joys began to gather around it like petals, reminding it that life still holds beauty waiting to be shaped.

This was the quiet gift the Porcupine carried: the knowing that even through sorrow, new expression can rise. Not to erase what has been lost, but to weave something tender and true from the threads that remain.

13
Coyote

Joker (4)
Wisdom & Folly

Coyote, aligned with the number 13, represents transformation through humour and trickery. It teaches you to find lightness and wisdom even in the darkest moments of grief, looking beyond your normal structures of life for levity, or having a break.

* **Opportunity:** Coyote offers the chance to see the humour in life's challenges and find unexpected insights, allowing you to adapt and heal.

* **Challenge:** The challenge is accepting that grief can be unpredictable and chaotic, yet it is part of the healing journey; to

not become stuck in negative feelings that constantly weigh you down. Do not maintain a routine and structure that is not serving your higher purpose.

Questions for today
How has grief made you feel tricked or misled? What habits can you adopt to regain trust in your life and yourself? What stability do you need to regain or create in order to move forward? What wisdom can you draw upon from your grief that will create empowering change in your transition? What negative thoughts is your inner voice telling you? How have you become stuck in your routines, what rigidity do you need to let go of?

Affirmation:
- "I embrace the lessons hidden within challenges and change."
- "I find humour and wisdom in life's challenges."

Self-Care Activity
Engage in playful activity – Coyote is famous for playing tricks and pranks on people. How can you surprise yourself or someone else and bring joy into their life today? Allow yourself to have fun by doing something light-hearted, such as playing a game or engaging in a creative hobby. Embracing playfulness can lighten your mood and bring joy. Keep finding a way forward, look at what work you need to do to help yourself.

Story
In ancient teachings, Coyote was revered as a creature of cleverness, adaptability, and resilience. Among many Indigenous cultures of North America, Coyote is a central figure in stories and teachings, often acting

as a trickster who challenges assumptions and offers lessons through humour and mischief. Its presence reminds us that life's challenges often carry hidden insights, and that navigating uncertainty can require both resourcefulness and a light heart.

Coyote thrives in diverse environments, a testament to the power of flexibility and perseverance. By observing its behaviour, we learn that healing is not always linear - there are missteps, surprises, and moments of reflection, each offering opportunities for growth. Stories of Coyote teach that cleverness and humour can be tools for transformation, helping us to face adversity with creativity and resilience.

In some Indigenous cultures, a coyote's appearance in the wild is considered an omen or a mystical sign. In some traditions, such as those of the Okanagan, Coyote is a transformer figure who helps bring order to the world or creates important elements of the natural world, like stars.

In Mexican traditions, Coyote is seen as a guide who bridges the human world with the spiritual realm, representing both cunning and wisdom. For Coyote to survive, he must look beyond the everyday, use wisdom from past mistakes, and do so by being able to laugh at himself, while also remaining grounded. Coyote has a wonderful 'work ethic', never giving up, always trying again to get what he needs or wants.

Coyote's way of moving through the world teaches that grief, like life itself, is unpredictable. By embracing uncertainty, learning from our experiences, and allowing space for levity even in difficult times, we cultivate resilience, insight, and a renewed sense of purpose.

Fable | Wisdom and Folly
The Coyote trotted along the edge of the desert at dusk, its paws stirring soft dust as the first stars appeared. Known for its cunning, it had walked between worlds - learning from every stumble. Once, it

tried to outrun its sorrow, seeking distraction, and only found stillness when it sat among the stones and felt the earth beneath its feet.

Grief, the Coyote realised, strips away what is not essential, leaving only the foundations that endure. Mistakes and missteps became lessons, each one strengthening the base upon which true resilience is built. Folly was no longer feared; each stumble reinforced the structure of its spirit.

One morning, it found a Fox weighed down by grief. "Why so burdened?" Coyote asked. The Fox sighed. "I thought I knew my path, but now nothing makes sense."

"Perhaps your path was a story you told yourself," Coyote said. "Grief clears away what is unstable. Build slowly, step by step, on what is real. Humour helps - not to escape, but to soften the load. Notice the small moments that steady your heart. Trust the process and honour the structure of your own spirit."

The Fox's eyes softened. "So grief isn't only an ending?"

"No," said Coyote. "It is the dismantling of what cannot endure, and the shaping of something firm, dependable, and true. Move deliberately, with care. When folly appears, consider if it is imposed by the world or your own mind."

The Fox rose slowly, the weight eased, and followed the Coyote into the rising sun. Healing, Coyote reminded those who crossed its trail, is not returning to what was, but rebuilding on a solid foundation, one step at a time, until your spirit stands strong and steady.

14
Dog

Loyalty (5)
The Power
of Loyalty

Dog's connection to the number 14 symbolises loyalty and balance. It encourages you to stay true to your values and relationships, even in times of grief. Remember to remain loyal to yourself before all others, for without that you cannot find freedom through changing times.

* **Opportunity:** Dog teaches the value of loyalty to yourself and those you love, building connection and support even in times of deep loss. Balance here is needed.

* **Challenge:** The challenge is not to isolate yourself or lose faith in relationships when grieving. Apathy towards others will not serve you.

Questions for today

Are you remaining loyal to your emotional needs? What daily ritual could reinforce your commitment to self-care? What discipline do you need to reinstate or instil to bring a sense of freedom? Have you been too devoted to helping others and not supporting yourself? Have you stayed loyal to outdated modes of thinking and feeling and not wanting to change? Have you questioned your loyalty to your faith and found this the most challenging aspect of all? Are you prepared to be true to yourself and risk disapproval of others?

Affirmation:

- "I remain loyal to my heart and those I love."
- "I embrace loyalty and support in my relationships."

Self-Care Activity

Have a think about what you are being loyal to now – is it yourself and your path, or that of another's? Has this served you? Allow yourself time to consider this and feel whatever emotions surface. Spend quality time with a loved one. Whether it's a friend, family member, or a pet, dedicating time to connect with someone you care about reinforces feelings of loyalty and support.

Story

In ancient teachings, Dog was revered as a creature of loyalty and protection, a faithful companion whose presence brought comfort and safety. Across many cultures, dogs have been honoured for their devotion to humans, guiding and supporting those around them while strengthening bonds of trust and care. Their presence reminds us that healing is nurtured through connection and the gentle power of love.

In Egyptian mythology, Anubis, the jackal-headed guardian of the dead, guided souls through the afterlife, embodying loyalty and protection during transitions between worlds. In Greek tradition, dogs were associated with Hecate, appearing as devoted companions who offered guidance and safeguarded those navigating uncertainty. Indigenous cultures also valued dogs for their companionship and attentiveness, teaching lessons of devotion, care, and emotional support.

Dog's way of moving through life teaches that loyalty is an active practice. By remaining faithful to ourselves and others, by offering protection and nurturing connection, we cultivate resilience and trust. Dogs show us that grief can be carried more gently when supported by love and steady presence, and that even in solitude, faithfulness to one's own values provides guidance and strength.

Fable | The Power of Loyalty
The Dog, steadfast and watchful, padded through a sunlit meadow, its ears alert to the whispers of the wind. Known for its loyalty and gentle guidance, it often drew strength from connection and presence. One morning, it noticed a young Deer standing quietly among the tall grass, shoulders heavy with sorrow.

"Why do you carry such a weight, friend?" the Dog asked, its voice calm yet attentive.

The Deer lowered its gaze. "Grief has left me unsure. I feel disconnected from those I care about, and even from myself." The Dog stepped closer, eyes warm. "Loyalty isn't just about standing by others. It begins within. Being true to your own heart allows you to navigate sorrow without losing yourself."

The Deer hesitated. "But how can I care for myself while feeling so pulled apart by loss?"

"Start by listening to your own needs," said the Dog gently. "Honor your feelings. Allow yourself to rest when necessary, and reach out when you need support. There is strength in asking for help, and freedom in recognising that connection doesn't diminish your independence."

The Deer's ears twitched, a hint of relief softening its stance. "So, I can still remain loyal to myself and to those I love?" "Exactly," the Dog affirmed. "True loyalty is a balance between honouring your heart and nurturing your bonds. Grief may test you, but when you walk with integrity and openness, you find resilience. You will discover that even in sorrow, trust, love, and loyalty can guide you forward."

The Deer lifted its head, feeling lighter, and together they moved through the meadow, companions in both grief and healing, guided by the steady wisdom of loyalty and the freedom to choose their path.

15
Wolf

Teacher (6)
The Pathfinder

Wolf, linked to the number 15, represents the teacher and inner wisdom. It guides you to learn from your grief, finding the lessons and strength within and with others around you that you are creating a nurturing path for you.

- **Opportunity:** Wolf provides the opportunity to learn valuable lessons from grief and to embrace wisdom through introspection.
- **Challenge:** The challenge is learning to trust your intuition and inner voice, especially when grief clouds your judgment.

Questions for today
What has grief taught you about yourself so far? How can you incorporate these lessons into your daily habits to create healing? What healthy boundaries may you need to make? What relationships have you been avoiding? Are you feeling taken advantage of due to your need to be responsible for everyone else? Have you separated yourself from your 'pack', believing you don't belong anymore? What emotion do you really need to let go of physically?

Affirmation:
- "I seek wisdom and guidance from my inner teacher."
- "I embrace the wisdom of my experiences."
- "I learn and grow from every experience, even in grief."

Self-Care Activity
Reflect and journal about a lesson learned. Take a few minutes to write about a recent experience and the lessons it has taught you. This helps integrate learning and promotes your personal growth. Consider the role you are playing in supporting others, and who else is supporting and nurturing you. If you have found yourself withdrawing and focused on yourself, a great self-care activity is to help guide others in their pain. Lived experience is a wonderful antidote. Play new music you have not heard of before – listen to new songs that have no past meaning for you.

Story
In ancient teachings, Wolf was honoured as a creature of instinct and guidance, moving through the world with both independence and connection. Among many Indigenous cultures of North America, Wolf is seen as a teacher, guiding people to trust their intuition while

remaining mindful of the bonds that tie communities together. Its presence reminds us that strength and wisdom are cultivated through both self-awareness and shared experience.

Wolves rely on their instincts to navigate complex landscapes, a reminder that trusting one's inner voice is essential, especially during times of grief and uncertainty. Living in tightly knit packs, wolves demonstrate the importance of relationships, mutual support, and collaboration in overcoming life's challenges. Their careful balance of independence and social cohesion teaches the value of self-reliance alongside attentive care for others.

In Norse mythology, Fenrir, the mighty wolf, represents the cycles of life and death, illustrating the necessity of both destruction and renewal. In Roman legend, the she-wolf who nurtured Romulus and Remus symbolises protection, guidance, and the quiet strength that underpins care for the young. Across these stories, wolves are revered as pathfinders and teachers, encouraging individuals to embrace their inner wisdom, act with courage, and maintain connection to those who journey alongside them.

The Wolf, a wise leader of its pack, guided its family through harsh winters and perilous situations. The Wolf shared its knowledge of survival and leadership, teaching the younger wolves the importance of teamwork and strategy. The pack thrived under the Wolf's guidance, and its role as a teacher was celebrated, symbolising the value of wisdom and the responsibility of sharing knowledge.

Fable | The Pathfinder
The Wolf moved confidently through the forest, its paws steady on the earth, eyes alert to every shadow and sound. Nearby, a solitary Snake observed, coiled quietly in the underbrush, watching the Wolf guide its pack.

The Wolf paused, then gestured with a tilt of its head toward the group. Every member had a role, some scouts, some nurturers, others protectors and a leader. Each wolf knew its place, yet all supported one another, their strengths balanced to create harmony and resilience. The pack thrived not because one wolf led alone, but because every individual's contribution mattered.

The Snake watched as the pack communicated silently with glances, posture, noises and subtle movements. Even the youngest members learned from the elders, growing in confidence and skill under careful guidance. The Wolf's leadership was not domination but stewardship, ensuring every wolf could flourish while maintaining the unity of the whole.

The Snake asked, "Why do you lead others when you could roam freely? Wouldn't you be more powerful alone?" The Wolf shook its head. "My power comes from the pack. Alone, I may be strong, but together, we are unstoppable. Solitude can teach wisdom, but connection shows the power of shared purpose. Grief may feel isolating yet support and guidance can help you navigate your path. Observe, learn, and when the time comes, step forward, carrying both your knowledge and the lessons of those who walked with you."

The Snake, who preferred solitude, considered this. It realised the importance of unity and teamwork. The Wolf's leadership taught all the animals that there is power in collaboration and that great things can be achieved when individuals work together toward a common goal.

Wolf's way of moving through the world teaches that healing is both a personal and communal path. By trusting our instincts, cultivating strong relationships, and leading with integrity, we learn to navigate grief with balance, insight, and a steady, enduring strength.

16
Raven

Magic (7)

The Messenger of Hidden Truths

Raven's connection to the number 16 represents transformation and the mystical. It encourages you to embrace the mysteries of life and trust in the magic of healing.

* **Opportunity:** Raven encourages you to embrace the mystery of life and the transformative power of loss, opening to spiritual insight.
* **Challenge:** The challenge is confronting the fear of the unknown and the uncertainty that grief often brings.

Questions for today

Are you open to the unexpected in your grief journey? What small change could you introduce today that might bring unexpected healing? Have you been outside at night to look at the stars and ponder life's greater mysteries? Or have you thought to research more about your energy fields? What magic are you denying in your life right now? What new way of thinking and learning might help you move forward and cope better? What mystery needs solving right now?

Affirmation:
- "I embrace the magic and mystery of transformation."
- "I trust in the magic of transformation and healing."

Self-Care Activity

Research a creative expression. Engage in a magical activity like drawing, writing, or crafting. Channelling your creativity can help you connect with the sense of wonder and magic in your life. Consider seeing a magic show. Learn more about something mysterious and mystifying; allow a new world to open up to you. Research something about the metaphysical plane.

Story

In ancient teachings, Raven was revered as a creature of insight and transformation, moving between the seen and unseen with grace and intelligence. Raven symbolises magic in many cultures; it is seen as a mediator between the physical world and the spiritual or unseen realms, carrying messages and insights that ordinary perception cannot grasp. Its intelligence, shape-shifting behaviour, and role in myths as a creator, trickster, or guide give it a mystical presence, representing transformation, mystery, and the power to influence unseen forces.

In Celtic mythology, Raven is closely associated with the goddess Morrigan, a figure of fate and change, guiding souls through the cycles of life and death. The birds symbolised her presence, acting as omens of death and messengers on the battlefield.

Ravens are known for their keen intelligence and resourcefulness, encouraging us to trust our instincts and remain aware of the subtle signs around us. In Norse mythology, Odin is accompanied by two ravens, Huginn (Thought) and Muninn (Memory), who journey across the world and return with knowledge. These stories highlight the raven's role as a messenger and guide, symbolising wisdom, foresight, and the careful attention needed to navigate complex experiences.

Raven's way of moving through the world teaches that healing requires both awareness and adaptability. By observing, reflecting, and listening to the lessons within our grief, we can gain clarity and insight, learning to transform loss into understanding and to approach life's uncertainties with wisdom and grace.

Fable | The Messenger of Hidden Truths
The Raven soared across the twilight sky, its black feathers catching the last light of the setting sun, glinting like shards of obsidian. The wind carried whispers of the unseen, and every shadow seemed alive with possibility. Below, a solitary ant paused, its tiny body dwarfed by the forest, yet its gaze lifted in wonder at the figure gliding above.

"Raven," the ant asked, "why do you dwell in the spaces where light fades and shadows deepen? What do you see that I cannot?"

The Raven circled slowly, its voice a melodic caw that seemed to vibrate through the very air. "In the places where the ordinary ends, magic begins. The unseen world holds secrets not meant for every eye. It is in silence, in patience, and in the willingness to look beyond the obvious that wisdom reveals itself. The mysteries of the forest, the shifting patterns of wind and leaf, the subtle movements of the stars—these are the lessons of the hidden realms."

The ant trembled slightly, feeling the weight of the Raven's presence. "But how can I trust what I cannot touch, or know what is real?"

The Raven's eyes glimmered, reflecting the faint light of the moon. "Trust comes from within. Look deeply, observe without fear, and let intuition guide you. Magic does not shout, it whispers. The unseen teaches those who listen, and every shadow holds a story waiting to unfold. Fear binds you; curiosity frees you. To embrace the unknown is to awaken the spirit."

The Raven spread its wings wide, casting a moving pattern of darkness and light across the forest floor. "See how the night folds around the world, how stars spark in secret places? That is the power of number seven—the seeker, the mystic, the bridge between worlds. In your own journey, grief may seem a darkness you cannot penetrate. Yet within it lies a hidden current, a path toward understanding, transformation, and insight. Follow the signs, no matter how small, and allow the magic of the unseen to guide you."

The ant, small and still, felt a shift within, as if the forest itself had whispered directly to its heart. The Raven lifted into the sky once more, leaving a trail of shimmering shadow in its wake. In its flight was a promise: that the mysteries, the magic, and the unseen truths are always available to those who dare to rise above fear and trust in the journey.

17
Mountain Lion

Leadership (8)
The Keeper of Courageous Vision

Mountain Lion, resonating with the number 17, symbolises leadership and responsibility. It teaches you to take charge of your healing journey with strength and courage.

* **Opportunity:** Mountain Lion helps you step into a position of self-leadership, guiding your way through grief with confidence.
* **Challenge:** The challenge is overcoming feelings of helplessness and taking charge of your healing process, thinking in the longer term about how you want to feel.

Questions for today
Are you leading your healing journey, or letting it lead you? How can you take charge of your grief process today? What investment must you make to help yourself move forward? If you are feeling lost, what dominating thoughts or people are limiting your power? What do you need to summon your courage to face? Who will support your new vision for your life? What long term plans do you need to revisit? What responsibility do you have to others'?

Affirmation:
- "I embrace my inner leader and navigate my path with confidence."
- "I lead my life with courage and integrity."

Self-Care Activity
Set a small goal and take action. Identify a manageable goal that you can work towards today and take a concrete step towards achieving it. This helps build confidence and reinforces your sense of leadership.

Story
In many Indigenous traditions of the Americas, the Mountain Lion is honoured as a powerful guardian and guide, moving through the world with quiet strength and purposeful intent.

Among Indigenous traditions of the Americas, it appears as Toho, a protective kachina spirit in Hopi and Zuni cultures, watching over the land and offering strength in times of danger. Its solitary, deliberate movements teach self-trust, showing that true power comes from clarity and acting with intention rather than impulse.

The Huichol people of Mexico regard the Mountain Lion as a being of ancestral fire and spiritual power, a reminder to walk with clarity and personal authority. These teachings portray the mountain lion as a quiet yet commanding presence, embodying the discipline and leadership needed to walk one's path.

Ancient teachings emphasise that true leaders possess quiet confidence, guiding others not through force but through understanding and empathy. They remind us that leadership often involves standing strong in the face of adversity and being willing to protect and nurture those who follow.

Fable | The Keeper of Courageous Vision
The Mountain Lion stood atop the ridge, golden fur glowing in the first light of dawn, eyes sharp, surveying the valley below. Its presence was both commanding and calm, a symbol of inner strength and leadership. Beneath, a busy Beaver paused from gathering wood, glancing up at the majestic cat.

"You are so quiet, Mountain Lion," Beaver said. "How do you lead without words?"

The Mountain Lion's gaze softened as it descended toward the riverbank. "Leadership is not in the loudest roar or the sharpest command," it replied. "True power comes from knowing yourself and trusting your instincts and guiding others with integrity. Every action, every choice, carries weight."

Beaver thought for a moment, considering its own frantic efforts. "But how do you inspire without telling others what to do?"

"By being present, by showing strength, and by standing in my own power," Mountain Lion said, pacing deliberately. "I have learned the balance between personal authority and the responsibility we hold to others. It is a reminder that our own confidence shapes the world around us. Grief can shake your foundations, but when you step fully into your power, you find clarity, direction, and the ability to rise above challenges."

Beaver lowered its head, realising how much it had tried to control every stick in its dam. "I see now," it said softly. "Perhaps leadership is as much about listening and observing as it is about doing."

Mountain Lion nodded, a silent acknowledgement of the lesson. "The path of leadership is steady and deliberate. Trust yourself, honour your strength, act with purpose and find that there is power there to guide you and others."

18
Lynx

Observation (9)

The Keeper
of Secrets

Lynx, aligned with the number 18, represents secrets, intuition and self-compassion. It guides you to trust your inner wisdom and the silent knowledge that comes from within during your grief journey.

* **Opportunity:** Lynx offers the chance to uncover hidden emotions and truths within yourself, promoting deep emotional healing.

* **Challenge:** The challenge is confronting buried feelings and allowing yourself to fully experience your grief without repression, but compassion.

Questions for today
What truths about your grief are you holding back? How can you safely express your hidden emotions today? Do you need to forgive yourself or others, or find more compassion? Are you feeling like you're learning more about others than yourself? What secrets have you been asked to keep that do not serve you? What secrets must you keep in honouring others? What are you observing and learning about others behaviours that will help you determine a path forward? What secrets have been shared with you that harm others?

Affirmation:
- "I uncover hidden truths and embrace the wisdom within."
- "I observe in silence."

Self-Care Activity
Create a personal space for reflection. Find a quiet spot where you can sit and reflect on your thoughts or secrets. Journaling or meditating in this space helps in understanding and embracing what's hidden within.

Story
In ancient teachings, Lynx is honoured as a guardian of secrets and a guide for introspection. In many Indigenous cultures of North America, its quiet, watchful presence encourages individuals to explore their hidden emotions and trust their inner voice. Observing the Lynx teaches that embracing our vulnerabilities can lead to strength and deeper understanding, supporting emotional healing through reflection and patience.

In some Slavic traditions, it is seen as a protector of the forest. Its presence encourages contemplation and trust in one's own knowledge, helping navigate uncertainty with clarity and calm.

By moving with stillness and purpose, Lynx teaches that healing does not require force or haste. Through quiet attentiveness and respect for our inner guidance, we can face grief and challenges with grace, gaining wisdom and confidence along the way.

Fable | The Keeper of Secrets
The Lynx moved silently through the forest, its fur blending seamlessly with the shadows, eyes glinting with quiet intelligence. Every step carried awareness; every pause was deliberate. In the heart of the woods, it discovered an intricate Spider weaving a delicate, shimmering web between the trees.

The Spider called out, "Lynx, your movements are almost invisible. How do you keep your knowledge and intentions so hidden?" The Lynx crouched, its gaze calm and measured. "There is power in discretion," it said. "Not all truths are meant for every ear. Some knowledge is sacred, entrusted only to those who seek it with honesty and clarity of heart. Secrets are threads in a vast web of understanding. Handle them with care, and they reveal wisdom beyond the surface."

The Spider shivered its silken legs in wonder. "But how do you know when to share and when to remain silent?"

"The timing is everything," the Lynx replied. "Some lessons come too soon; some truths need patience to be understood. Like the Spider's web, the threads of knowledge must be strong and precise. Share only what strengthens, only what heals, and the rest remains hidden, protecting both the giver and the seeker."

The Spider watched, feeling the weight of responsibility in every shimmering thread. "So, silence can be a gift?"

"Indeed," said the Lynx, stepping lightly onto a moss-covered rock. "Many truths shared speak of completion and insight, of spiritual awareness and selflessness. In grief, there are times to speak and times to hold sacred space. Honouring secrets, yours or another's, teaches compassion, patience, love and discernment. This is the hidden power, guiding those who are willing to see beyond the surface." The Spider nodded, inspired that not all knowledge needs to be spoken, and there is great strength in knowing when to remain silent.

19
Buffalo

Gratitude (1)

Guardian of Gratitude
and Abundance

Buffalo's connection to the number 19 represents leadership, prayer, abundance, and gratitude. It encourages you to remain thankful for the blessings in your life, even amidst grief.

* **Opportunity:** Buffalo reminds you to connect with gratitude and abundance in life, even when surrounded by loss, nurturing spiritual connection.

* **Challenge:** The challenge is to avoid focusing solely on what has been lost, opening yourself to receive blessings still present.

Questions for today

Are you tapping into gratitude amidst your grief? What can you be grateful for today, no matter how small? What new approaches could you take to support your new individual path forward? Have you been waiting on other people to help you only to be let down? How are you role modelling healing behaviours for those that look up to you? What abundance surrounds you that you have forgotten to acknowledge recently?

Affirmation:
- "I connect with abundance and gratitude through prayer."
- "I am grateful for the abundance in my life."

Self-Care Activity

Practice gratitude. Take a moment to list five things you are grateful for. This practice can shift your focus towards abundance and build a sense of well-being and contentment. Take the one gratitude item that makes you feel the most in your heart, then list five reasons why you feel grateful for that in your life. Sit or walk while you think about why you truly feel grateful for this and let it radiate from your heart out into the Universe.

Story

In many indigenous cultures, the Buffalo is revered as a symbol of abundance and gratitude. The Native American tribes of the Great Plains view the Buffalo as a sacred animal. It was necessary for their way of life and survival. They are integral to various ceremonies, such as the Buffalo Dance, which is performed to honour and thank the Buffalo for their sustenance and the abundance it brings. The animal is believed to carry the energy of Mother Earth and is associated with spiritual strength and resilience.

They believe that honouring the Buffalo and expressing gratitude for its gifts such as food, clothing, and shelter brings blessings and abundance to the community. The teachings emphasise that, like the Buffalo, we should remain steadfast and grateful, recognising that even in times of hardship, there are blessings to be found that sustain us on our journey.

Indigenous cultures teach that gratitude for the Buffalo's gifts can lead to greater abundance in life. This is reflected in the concept of the "Buffalo Woman" or "White Buffalo Calf Woman," who is seen as a messenger of peace and abundance, bringing teachings of respect and gratitude. The White Buffalo is thought to represent Miracles.

Fable | Guardian of Gratitude and Abundance
The Buffalo roamed the plains, bringing abundance and sustenance to its fellow creatures. During a severe drought, the Buffalo led the herd to a hidden source of water and fertile ground, ensuring their survival. Its role in providing for the community and the prayers of gratitude it received symbolised the abundance and blessings of life, teaching the power of generosity and faith.

Buffalo stood proudly on the sunlit plains, its massive form radiating strength and presence. Every step pressed lightly into the earth, yet carried the weight of wisdom. A small Hare approached, wary yet curious.

"Buffalo," the Hare whispered, "you are so strong and steady. How do you always seem to have enough, even when the land changes?"

Buffalo lowered its head and exhaled slowly, a warm rumble vibrating through the grass. "I do not cling to scarcity," it said. "I give thanks for each blade of grass, each breath of wind, each drop of rain, each touch of sunlight. Gratitude opens the way to abundance. When you honour the gifts of Mother Earth, life provides what is needed."

The Hare twitched its ears nervously. "But what if the world takes more than it gives? What if I lose what I hold dear?"

Buffalo lifted its eyes, calm and deep as the horizon. "Loss is part of the journey. Yet even in grief, there is abundance, memories, love, lessons, and courage. By acknowledging what you have, even when it seems small, you invite more into your life. Gratitude is the first step to reclaiming joy and strength."

From that day, the Hare moved through the plains differently. It noticed the sun on its fur, the wind in the grass, and the quiet generosity of the world around it. Buffalo's teachings echoed through the land: abundance flows to those who live with gratitude, honour the Earth, and recognise the blessings in every moment.

20
Mouse

Scrutiny (2)
Keeper of Detail
and Awareness

Mouse, resonating with the number 20, symbolises sensitivity, scrutiny and attention to detail. It encourages you to be mindful of the small steps and changes in your healing process.

* **Opportunity:** Mouse teaches the value of closely examining the details of your emotions, helping you identify the small steps needed for healing. The opportunity is to find balance in your activities that support your emotional journey, balancing the need for deep feeling and light-heartedness.

* **Challenge:** The challenge is to not get lost in the minutiae and lose sight of the bigger picture of healing, or feeling overly-sensitive to anyone's suggestions for how you might move forward.

Questions for today
Are you getting lost in the details of grief? What daily practice can help you zoom out and see the bigger picture? Are you feeling highly reactive to everyone's words around you? Do you need to finalise some contracts or paperwork that requires scrutiny? Have you been a bit touchy generally? Do you need to look more closely at the details in your life – have you let things go that need attention? Are you caught up in details that do not matter anymore and can you make new meaning with them?

Affirmation:
- "I observe and understand my sensitivities."
- "I pay attention to the details of my healing journey."

Self-Care Activity
Organise a small area of your life. Tidy up a space like your desk or a drawer. This small act of organisation can provide clarity and a sense of control, reflecting the careful scrutiny associated with the Mouse. Pack away things that make you feel sad or cluttered in your mind. Take some time out to let all the sensitive emotions come out in whatever way they need, and balance this with a positive mindset. Turn your phone off, disconnect and give yourself space to feel.

Story
In many Indigenous cultures, the Mouse is seen as a symbol of keen observation and awareness. It teaches the importance of paying attention to the details in our environment and emotions, emphasising that small, seemingly insignificant actions can lead to significant outcomes. This aligns with the idea that introspection and mindfulness are essential for personal growth and healing.

The Mouse also embodies resourcefulness, often using its surroundings to create safety and sustenance. This reflects teachings that encourage individuals to utilise their resources wisely and adapt to their circumstances. The ability to make the most out of limited resources is a valuable life skill that is celebrated across various cultures.

Fable | Keeper of Detail and Awareness
Mouse scurried along the forest floor, whiskers twitching at every sound, noticing the smallest movements in the grass and the tiniest seeds hidden in the soil. From above, Crow watched, its black feathers gleaming in the sunlight.

"Mouse," Crow called down, wings spread wide, "you are always so focused on the tiniest details. Why do you spend so much time on such small things?"

Mouse paused, looking up with bright, alert eyes. "Because the small things matter," it replied. "If I do not pay attention, I might miss the seeds I need to survive, or the dangers that are quietly creeping closer. Life is built on these small, essential pieces."

Crow tilted its head thoughtfully. "But does focusing on the small things ever blind you to the bigger world?"

Mouse twitched its whiskers, considering. "Sometimes," it admitted, "but without care for the details, the bigger picture cannot hold together. Both must exist, awareness of the small and understanding of the whole. One strengthens the other."

Crow cawed softly, circling higher above the trees. "You teach me patience and precision, Mouse. Even in grief, your careful eyes remind us to notice what might otherwise be lost, the quiet joys, the small lessons, the subtle gifts hidden in sorrow."

Mouse nodded. "And you remind me to lift my gaze, to see the wider path of my journey. Together, we balance one another, blending scrutiny with perspective. Even in darkness, there is clarity when we honour both the detail and the whole."

From that day, the animals of the forest learned that wisdom comes from combining focus and vision, that attention to detail enriches understanding, and that being mindful of the small things can illuminate even the heaviest hearts.

21
Owl

Silent Wisdom (3)

Keeper of
Silent Wisdom

Owl, aligned with the number 3, embodies insight and the power of expression. It invites you to trust your inner voice, share your thoughts openly, and communicate with clarity even in challenging moments. Through its watchful presence, Owl encourages creativity, joy, and connection, helping you see opportunities for growth and understanding that might otherwise remain hidden.

* **Opportunity:** Owl brings the chance to see through illusions, helping you gain clarity and wisdom in the face of grief. It brings forth an opportunity to explore beyond your immediate

surroundings for help, to see and more importantly, hear messages coming through in a range of ways to support you right now.

- **Challenge:** The challenge is recognising self-deception or denial in your grief process, confronting hard truths.

Questions for today

Are you being honest with yourself about your grief? What daily action could help you uncover your true feelings? Are you surrounding yourself with too many people and not focusing on your own inner wisdom and knowing? Have you lost your creative spark to see a way forward? Is there too much 'noise' in your environment that you cannot hear things clearly?

Affirmation:

- "I seek creative ways forward based on my observations."
- "I see through deception and find clarity in my path."

Self-Care Activity

Seek clarity. Spend some time researching or gently asking questions about something that feels unclear or deceptive in your life. Gaining more information can help you see through illusions and gain a clearer perspective. Head out at night to see if you can spot some owls!

Story

In many cultures, this silent guardian is associated with wisdom and the ability to see beyond illusions. In ancient Egyptian mythology, it was revered as a symbol of protection and insight, believed to guide souls through the afterlife. Similarly, in Native American traditions, it is seen as a messenger of secrets, urging individuals to trust their intuition. Athena, the Greek Goddess of wisdom and warfare, embodies the qualities of this creature, symbolising the strength that comes from knowledge and self-reflection. Just as she guided heroes through challenges, this guardian teaches that seeking inner clarity can illuminate the path through grief.

In Tarot, Owl is linked to the High Priestess, a card embodying intuition, mystery, secrets and hidden knowledge. Like the High Priestess, the guardian teaches the importance of looking within for answers and trusting one's inner wisdom.

The Moon card in tarot often represents the opportunity to seek clarity amidst grief, as it encourages exploration of the subconscious, even though it can also signify deception and illusions, prompting us to delve into our hidden emotions and potentially confront difficult truths during times of sorrow.

Owls, with their silent flight and exceptional hunting skills, offer profound insights into grief recovery. Just as the Owl's feathers enable it to navigate the darkness without a sound, those experiencing grief can learn to move through their emotional landscape quietly and introspectively, allowing themselves to explore the depths of their feelings without the noise of external expectations.

The Owl's acute hearing symbolises the importance of tuning into one's inner voice and intuition, guiding individuals to uncover hidden emotions and truths that may need attention. By embracing the Owl's patience and stealth, one can approach the healing journey with the same quiet determination, acknowledging that healing often requires a delicate balance of reflection and action, much like the Owl's strategic approach to hunting. This connection encourages individuals to honour their grief while remaining open to the transformative wisdom that arises from within.

Fable | Keeper of Silent Wisdom

Owl perched high in the ancient oak, feathers soft as moonlight, eyes luminous with quiet knowing. Below, Porcupine padded through the underbrush, alert yet unaware of the watcher above.

"You move so silently," Porcupine murmured, looking up. "How do you see so much while being so quiet?"

Owl's head turned slowly, eyes gleaming. "Wisdom does not need words," it said. "In silence, we hear what is otherwise hidden. The heart, the unseen, the whispered truths, all reveal themselves when we listen without speaking."

Porcupine frowned. "But how can you guide others, or understand their struggles, without talking?"

"Words can distract," Owl replied, casting shadows across the forest floor. "They can hide as much as they reveal. Sometimes, people deceive themselves with too much talking. Silence reveals what lies beneath. It lets others show their true selves, whether in honesty or deception." Porcupine considered this, realising that perhaps it had spent too much time relying on its own voice rather than listening to the quiet around it.

True insight comes when you watch, when you notice the subtle shifts in energy, in emotion, in intention. Silence teaches patience, attention, and understanding beyond what can be spoken.

Porcupine paused, feeling the weight of grief it had carried alone. "So, even in sorrow, silence can show me the way?" Owl spread its wings softly. "Yes. Grief speaks in quiet rhythms. By listening, by observing the small signs, the rustle of leaves, the tilt of a branch, the stillness around you, you can discover your own answers. In mystery lies clarity, in stillness lies healing."

22
Beaver

Industriousness (22)

The Builder
of Dreams

Beaver, resonating with the master number 22, symbolises building and practicality. It encourages you to construct a strong foundation for your healing journey, focusing on resilience and practicality.

* **Opportunity:** Beaver encourages you to actively rebuild your life and structure after loss, through patience and hard work.
* **Challenge:** The challenge is overcoming stagnation or reluctance to begin again after grief.

Questions for today

How are you rebuilding your life after loss? What practical steps can you take today to strengthen your foundation? How are you role modelling healing to those around you and in your community? Have you let go of your dreams or feel the need to create new ones? What do you want to manifest in this next chapter in your life? Have you been focusing too much on what you don't have and need to think more about what you actually want moving forward? Have you become too caught up in your own 'busyness', to allow time to heal and process?

Affirmation:

- "I build a strong foundation for my healing and growth."
- "I create a foundation of strength and resilience."

Self-Care Activity

Start and complete a small, manageable project around your home or work. The sense of accomplishment from building something can be incredibly satisfying and empowering. Invite others to join you in your project.

Story

In various cultures, the Beaver is revered as a symbol of productivity and determination. Native American traditions often view the Beaver as a guardian of water, representing the flow of emotions and the importance of nurturing our inner selves. This connection emphasises the significance of creating balance in life, much like the Beaver creates harmony in its ecosystem. Beaver is indeed the Master Builder, able to create dams where Mother Nature needs them most – and they don't require permits to build; they intuitively know their ecosystem and where the water needs to flow. Building in this way allows them to support all plant life and animal life that live in harmony with nature. They do this as a team, helping each other and never stopping until it is complete, such is their industriousness.

In Tarot, the card associated with the number 22 is The Fool, which is sometimes numbered as 0 in the Major Arcana but can also be placed at the end of the sequence as 22. The Fool resonates with the idea of laying a strong foundation for new endeavours, encouraging resilience, creativity, and the courage to manifest dreams into reality. Just as the Beaver constructs its home with intention, it also creates a great foundation for The Fool that urges us to embark on our journeys with an open heart and a willingness to embrace the unknown. By embracing the beaver's qualities, we can cultivate resilience and creativity, paving the way for new beginnings.

Fable | The Builder of Dreams
Beaver worked tirelessly by the riverbank, its sharp teeth gnawing through the wood as it gathered supplies for its dam. Water trickled and pooled around its creation, each stick and branch forming a path of life. Overhead, Eagle soared, wings spread wide, watching the river and its diligent architect.

"You work hard, Beaver," Eagle called down. "But why do you spend so much time building? Couldn't you just find shelter somewhere else?" Beaver paused, looking up at Eagle's majestic wings. "I build not just for shelter, but for creation. My dam shapes the river's flow, creating new pools, homes for fish, and spaces for others to thrive."

Eagle circled lower. "But it takes so much effort. Don't you tire of the work?"

Beaver smiled. "The effort is part of the joy, Eagle. By building, I'm not just making a home, I'm shaping the world around me. Every branch I place changes the river's course, just as every action we take shapes the lives of others." Eagle swooped down, perching on a nearby rock. "Perhaps there is something to your method, Beaver. I see now that creation is not just about the result, but the journey of building it."

Beaver nodded, returning to its work. The animals of the forest learned from Beaver that hard work and persistence build not only shelter but entire ecosystems. Every action taken is a step toward creating something greater than oneself.

Beaver teaches us that even the smallest acts of care and focus can build foundations of lasting impact. Beaver's fable reminds us that grief, like the river, can be redirected, and through steady work, patience, and intention, we can shape new paths and nurture life in ourselves and others.

23
Opossum

Diversion (5)

The Art of Diversion

Opossum's connection to the number 23 represents adaptability and cleverness. It teaches you to find creative ways to navigate your grief, using flexibility to protect your heart.

* **Opportunity:** Opossum offers the gift of adaptability, teaching you to shift perspectives and find new paths when overwhelmed by grief.

* **Challenge:** The challenge is avoiding avoidance behaviours or diversions that prevent true healing from grief.

Questions for today

Are you distracting yourself from your grief, or facing it? What habit could help you confront your emotions in a healthy way? Have you discovered a range of new ways that could assist you in your journey? What new people or experiences have you had that you can tap into to move forward? What risks do you need to take to move forward in your healing? Are you easily diverted from your new path and being swept back into the past?

Affirmation:
- "I embrace solutions and adapt to changes."
- "I am flexible and solve problems creatively."

Self-Care Activity

Take a break and do something unexpected, like put on some music and dance at home. Go for a walk in a new place, sign up to a lesson in something different, try a new food or add some spice to your food! Changing your routine can provide a refreshing diversion and help you see things from a different perspective.

Story

In many indigenous cultures, the Opossum is viewed as a symbol of strategy and survival. Its ability to play dead is seen as a metaphor for the importance of choosing when to engage with challenges and when to retreat and reflect. The Opossum teaches the value of flexibility and adaptability, encouraging individuals to embrace life's uncertainties with humour and grace.

Additionally, in folklore, the opossum is associated with wisdom gained through experience. It reminds us that vulnerability can be a source of strength, and that survival often requires a blend of cunning and courage. In this way, it embodies the spirit of transformation, guiding us to navigate grief with the understanding that, just as it plays dead to avoid danger, we too can take moments to pause, reflect, and regroup as we journey through life's challenges.

Fable | The Art of Diversion
Opossum moved carefully through the tall grass, its eyes alert, tail swishing lightly with each step. Coyote watched from a distance, intrigued by its deliberate movements.

"You always move so cautiously," Coyote said. "Why not confront challenges directly?"

Opossum paused and looked calmly at Coyote. "Grief is like shifting wind. To face it all at once is to risk being swept away. I move with it, step by step, redirecting my energy and choosing the moments I engage. Sometimes the strongest way forward is not force, but flow."

Coyote tilted his head. "So, you avoid your grief?"

"Not avoid," Opossum replied. "I adapt. I shift, I change course when needed. In the spaces between action and stillness, I find balance. Life and grief are always in motion, and by embracing that movement, I allow healing to unfold naturally." Coyote watched quietly. "It seems you turn challenge into opportunity."

"Yes," said Opossum. "Change is a companion, not an enemy. By moving with the energy of life, letting go, diverting, exploring new paths, I remain resilient. Each shift teaches me about flexibility, freedom, change and discovering strength I didn't know I had."

The other animals soon noticed. Opossum's wisdom showed that grief is not something to battle head-on, but a force to navigate with creativity, courage, and adaptability. Through diversion and the willingness to flow with change, one can transform grief into growth and resilience.

24
Crow

Law (6)
The Law-Keeper

Crow, resonating with the number 24, symbolises law and balance for healing. It encourages you to respect the natural laws of life, death, and rebirth, finding peace in their inevitability.

* **Opportunity:** Crow helps you understand the universal laws of change and transformation, guiding you to accept loss as a natural part of life.
* **Challenge:** The challenge is letting go of resistance to change and accepting the transformative nature of grief.

Questions for today
What unspoken rules are you following in your grief? How can you challenge these to better support your healing? Are you feeling like a victim through the actions of others or rules you don't care for? Are you trying to control everyone around you? Have you been judging yourself or others too harshly? Do you need to attend to legal matters more promptly? What family issues require a resolution? What has fallen out of harmony in your life?

Affirmation:
- "I honour the laws of nature and align with universal truths."
- "I intrinsically know what is right for me in this time and place."

Self-Care Activity
Reflect daily on actions that maintain your inner balance. If anything is not working for you anymore, consider replacing it with a new activity. Give support wisely, without compromising your well-being.

Story
In ancient teachings, Crow is honoured as a messenger and a symbol of intelligence and transformation. They are believed to have the ability to navigate the worlds between the living and the dead, symbolising the transition between different states of being. This association with transformation encourages individuals to embrace change and view it as a necessary part of growth. Known for their problem-solving abilities, Crows embody intelligence and adaptability. In folklore, they are often depicted as clever tricksters, using their wits to navigate challenges. This symbolism reminds us to embrace our own intelligence and creativity when faced with obstacles.

In Chinese culture, the three-legged Crow (*Jinwu* – Golden Crow) is associated with the sun and is sometimes seen as a symbol of good fortune. In Hindu culture, Crows are seen as carriers of souls and are often associated with the ancestors (*Pitrs*). During rituals (*Sraddha* and *Pitrpaksa*), offerings are made to Crows to honour deceased loved ones, symbolising a connection to the spirit world and the continuity of life.

In various African cultures, Crows are seen as symbols of wisdom and protection. They are often associated with ancestral spirits and are believed to have the ability to communicate messages from the other side.

In Japanese mythology, the *Yatagarasu* is a three-legged crow (*Karasu*) considered a divine guide sent by the sun goddess Amaterasu to guide the first emperor, Jimmu, and is a symbol of guidance, divine will, and protection, particularly in the Kumano region. In Celtic mythology, the Crow (and raven) is associated with the Goddess Morrigan, often shown as a shapeshifter that can take the form of the Crow. She is often depicted with Crows and when they are seen are omens of her presence and her ability to influence the outcome of battles. She is also through the Crow, thought to bring messages of transformation and to guide souls in their journeys.

Crow's way of moving through the world teaches that transformation is a process of attentive observation and conscious choice. By paying close attention to what surrounds us, reflecting on our experiences, and remaining adaptable, we can navigate grief and challenges with clarity, intelligence, and resilience.

Fable | The Law Keeper

Crow perched high in the old oak, its sharp eyes scanning the forest with unwavering focus. Below, Tiger padded silently through the underbrush, muscles rippling with strength and curiosity.

"Crow, you watch everything so carefully," Tiger said, tilting its head. "What are you searching for?"

Crow ruffled its feathers, letting the breeze whisper through its wings. "I watch to keep balance. I observe where harmony falters and ensure that life's natural order is respected."

Tiger, proud and independent, growled softly. "But you're only one bird. How can you uphold the law of the forest?"

Crow's eyes gleamed with quiet authority. "It is not force that holds the law but understanding. Every action has its echo. By remembering and observing, I guide the forest without needing to strike. Justice is built into the world itself."

Tiger paused, considering this. "So, you don't punish. You let the forest correct itself?"

"Yes," Crow replied. " Nature takes care of that. I am simply the messenger, the observer. The law is in the very fabric of the world. Those who break it must face its consequences. My role is to illuminate the path, to remind others of their responsibility, helping the forest return to harmony."

Tiger's ears twitched. "Even in sorrow, when grief makes the world feel unsteady?"

"Especially then," Crow said. "Grief can cloud judgement and tempt one into impulsive action. By observing and acting with care, you restore inner balance. Harmony begins within, and through that, the world around you will find its rhythm again."

The animals of the forest came to understand Crow's quiet authority. It was not only a keeper of Law but a teacher of responsibility, showing that balance and careful observation are the foundations of resilience, especially when navigating the storms of grief.

25
Fox

Camouflage (7)

Master of Camouflage

Fox's connection to the number 25 represents adaptability and subtlety. It teaches you to navigate your grief with grace, blending into your surroundings as needed for protection.

* **Opportunity:** Fox provides the chance to adapt and blend into new environments, helping you find balance amidst the upheaval of grief.

* **Challenge:** The challenge is avoiding emotional withdrawal or hiding from grief instead of confronting it.

Questions for today
Are you hiding your emotions from others? How can you reveal more of your true feelings in your daily interactions? What can you learn about your emotional depths? Have you been feeling cornered with no way out? Do you need to create another strategy to move away from situations or people that no longer serve your best needs? What requires more research before you make a decision and can you do this without announcing it to everyone?

Affirmation:
- "I adapt and find my way through the mysteries of life with grace."
- "I can take a back seat to let others' shine."

Self-Care Activity
Practice mindfulness. Spend a few minutes focusing on your breath and being present in the moment. You can try this while walking, slowing down and really noticing what is around you. This practice helps you adapt to your surroundings and manage your emotions effectively. Try alternate nostril breathing, which can induce engagement with your pineal gland, opening up the possibility of wonderful visions.

Story
Across various cultures, the Fox embodies the teachings of adaptability, cleverness, and emotional resilience. It encourages individuals to navigate their grief with grace, blending into new environments while also revealing their true selves when necessary. These ancient teachings remind us that embracing our emotional journey, through both solitude and connection, can lead to healing and renewal.

In various Native American cultures, the Fox is often seen as a symbol of cleverness, adaptability, furtiveness and trickery. The Fox teaches the importance of wisdom and finding one's way through challenges with grace and agility. It is regarded as a teacher, reminding us to stay alert and aware of our surroundings while navigating the complexities of life, especially in times of grief.

Fable | Master of Camouflage
Fox darted through the forest, its red fur blending seamlessly with the autumn leaves. As it moved silently, it passed Rabbit, who was trembling beneath a bush. "Fox, how do you move so effortlessly without being seen?" Rabbit asked, its voice shaking with fear.

Fox grinned, its sharp teeth glinting in the sunlight. "It's all about blending in, Rabbit. I become part of the environment, and no one notices me." Rabbit's eyes widened. "But what if someone does notice you?"

Fox's eyes sparkled. "Then I simply become something else. I adapt to the situation—whether through stealth, speed, or wit. Camouflage isn't just about hiding, Rabbit. It's about knowing when to show yourself and when to disappear."

Rabbit nodded, still trembling. "But I'm always so afraid of being seen." Fox softened its expression. "Fear can be useful, but you must learn to use it wisely. By observing and adapting, you can blend in too. Not everything is a threat." From that day forward, Rabbit learned to observe its surroundings more carefully, realising that fear and camouflage could work together. Fox taught the animals that blending in with one's environment was not just about hiding, but about adaptability and awareness of the world around them.

26
Squirrel

Gathering (8)
Gathering with Purpose

Squirrel, aligned with the number 26, symbolises gathering and preparation. It encourages you to collect the emotional and spiritual resources you need for your healing journey.

* **Opportunity:** Squirrel encourages gathering the emotional resources and support systems needed for healing, planning for long-term recovery.
* **Challenge:** The challenge is to avoid hoarding or holding onto emotions that hinder the grief process.

Questions for today

Are you gathering support around you during your grief? What small step can you take today to reach out for help? What longer term view of yourself would you like to see come to light? Have you been hoarding money and not investing in yourself? Have you been spending too much money as a way to distract yourself? Are you more focused with material possession and what you can get, rather than what you are giving?

Affirmation:
- "I gather and cherish the resources I need for my healing."
- "I gather the resources I need for my healing journey."

Self-Care Activity

Organise your resources, including your finances. Working out clear budgets is a great form of self-care. Gather and organise items or information you need, whether it's planning meals, scheduling tasks, or arranging your workspace. This act of gathering can bring a sense of preparedness and calm.

Story

Across various cultures, the Squirrel embodies the teachings of gathering, preparation, and resourcefulness. It encourages individuals to collect the emotional and spiritual support needed for healing while cautioning against hoarding feelings or resources that may impede progress. These ancient teachings remind us that both community and self-care are vital as we navigate the complexities of grief and recovery.

In many Native American cultures, the Squirrel is seen as a symbol of preparedness and resourcefulness. It teaches the importance of gathering resources, both physical and emotional, to ensure survival and prosperity. The Squirrel's diligent work ethic encourages individuals to plan for the future while reminding them to be aware of their needs and to seek support from their community.

In Chinese folklore, squirrels symbolise energy and vitality. Their gathering behaviour reflects the idea of preparing for the future and the need to nurture oneself during difficult times. In some Asian cultures, squirrels are associated with good luck and prosperity, and their presence is seen as a positive omen.

Squirrels teach individuals to balance their desires with practicality, emphasising the importance of being resourceful in the face of challenges, particularly in emotional recovery.

Fable | Gathering with Purpose
Squirrel scampered up and down the tree branches, gathering acorns and stashing them away for the winter, carefully in hidden caches. Nearby, Raccoon watched with curiosity in its eyes. "Why are you always gathering, Squirrel? Don't you ever rest?" Raccoon asked. Squirrel paused, holding an acorn gently. "I gather to ensure I am ready for the future. Each acorn is a step toward security; a foundation I can rely on."

"But what if you collect too much? Isn't there a limit?" Raccoon wondered. "There is a balance," Squirrel replied. "I take what I need, but I also leave some behind for others. Some acorns I forget, and they grow into trees, creating abundance for the forest. Preparation and generosity go hand in hand."

Raccoon nodded slowly. "So, gathering isn't just for yourself?"

"No," Squirrel said with a wise twitch of its tail. "It's about creating stability and abundance and sharing what we can. In life and in grief, preparation allows us to weather storms, and generosity reminds us that even in loss, we can support others and help life flourish." The forest learned from Squirrel that careful preparation, balanced with generosity, creates resilience, abundance, and hope, even in times of sorrow.

27
Dragonfly

Illusion (9)
Illusion and Perception

Dragonfly's connection to the number 27 represents illusion and transformation. It teaches you to look beyond the surface and embrace the deeper truths in your grief journey.

* **Opportunity:** Dragonfly encourages you to break through illusions of grief and find clarity in what is real and true in your emotions.
* **Challenge:** The challenge is overcoming denial or the tendency to escape the painful realities of loss.

Questions for today
What illusions or expectations about grief are you holding onto? How can you create space for clarity in your daily habits? How can you better learn to let go of emotions that are keeping you stuck or disempowering you? Who do you need to forgive that will support your personal transformation? What perceptions do you need to change about yourself to move forward with compassion?

Affirmation:
- "I see through illusions and embrace clarity and truth."
- "I see beyond to the truth of my soul."

Self-Care Activity
Spend some time reflecting on your thoughts and feelings to discern what may be illusions or misconceptions. Journaling or meditating can help clarify and address any misleading beliefs.

Story
In ancient teachings, Dragonfly is honoured as a symbol of transformation and lightness. Across many Indigenous cultures, dragonflies are admired for their ability to move gracefully through air and water. Air represents the mental realm and perspective and the ability to rise above situations, while water reflects emotion and intuition. Dragonfly's movement between these elements reminds us to navigate life's changes with balance, openness, and emotional awareness.

Dragonflies are associated with clarity and self-realisation, showing that transformation involves seeing ourselves and our experiences more clearly. In Japanese culture, dragonflies symbolise courage, strength, and happiness, reinforcing the idea that embracing change can bring insight and renewal.

Through ancient stories and connections to deities, the Dragonfly serves as a powerful reminder of the potential for growth and healing, even in the face of grief. In some aspects of Celtic lore, Dragonflies are associated with the fae, or fairy folk, and that Dragonflies could serve as messengers between the realms of the living and the spirit world. Their iridescent wings are seen as magical, symbolising the connection to the otherworldly and the transformative nature of life and death.

In Hinduism, the Dragonfly could be considered appropriate to associate with the Goddess Durga, a powerful warrior Goddess who embodies strength and protection. The Dragonfly's ability to navigate both land and water reflects the Goddess's qualities of adaptability and resilience in the face of adversity. This connection reinforces the idea of finding strength within oneself during times of change.

Dragonfly's way of moving through the world teaches that healing grows from awareness and openness to change. By observing life with clarity and balancing thought with emotion, we can navigate grief and challenges with insight and renewed perspective.

Fable | Seeing Beyond Illusion
Dragonfly hovered gracefully above the shimmering pond, its wings reflecting every colour of the rainbow. Nearby, Frog watched from a lily pad, mesmerised by Dragonfly's movements.

"Dragonfly, you shift with the light," Frog said, tilting his head. "One moment you are here, the next you are gone. How do you move so effortlessly between what is and what seems?" Dragonfly's wings fluttered, sending tiny ripples across the water. "It's the nature of perception, Frog. What appears to be real is only part of the story. Life contains layers, and sometimes we must look beyond the surface to understand it fully."

Frog hesitated. "But isn't it confusing to question everything we see?"

"Not if you embrace it with patience," Dragonfly replied. "Illusions remind us that clarity comes with reflection. Grief, like my wings, can feel fleeting and shifting, but beneath the surface lies a deeper understanding. By accepting change and seeing beyond the immediate, we can find compassion for ourselves and others."

Frog nodded slowly. "So, even when I feel lost, there is meaning beneath the surface?"

"Exactly," Dragonfly said, hovering close. "Illusion teaches awareness. It invites us to pause and uncover truths that guide healing. In grief, perception may shift, but the journey leads to understanding, compassion, transformation and forgiveness."

The animals learned from Dragonfly that life and loss are rarely simple. By looking beyond illusion and embracing reflection, they could discover hidden truths, cultivate empathy, and navigate grief with deeper insight.

28
Armadillo

Boundaries (1)

The Guardian
of Boundaries

Armadillo, aligned with the number 28, represents boundaries and protection. It encourages you to set clear and healthy boundaries leading you in your grief to protect your emotional well-being.

* **Opportunity:** Armadillo helps you set healthy emotional boundaries, allowing you to protect your energy during the grief process.
* **Challenge:** The challenge is learning to say "no" and avoiding overextending yourself emotionally while grieving.

Questions for today

Are you setting healthy boundaries while you grieve? What is one boundary you can establish today to protect your emotional well-being? Who do you need to say 'No' to? How can you build your confidence for greater independence? Have you created too many boundaries and have isolated yourself from others to your detriment? Have you come to rely too much on others and not enough on yourself? Have you relinquished your independence and allowed everyone to tell you what you should do, how you should feel and what you should think?

Affirmation:

- "I establish and maintain healthy boundaries for my well-being."
- "I confidently enforce boundaries that protect myself."

Self-Care Activity

Create a personal sanctuary. Designate a special space in your home where you can retreat and relax. This area serves as a boundary to protect your well-being and offers a retreat from stress.

Story

The Armadillo's teachings on boundaries resonate deeply with the grief journey. By honouring its instincts to protect itself, the armadillo reminds us that establishing healthy emotional boundaries is vital for navigating the complexities of loss. Embracing the strength to say "no" when necessary and recognising the value of self-care can lead to profound healing and growth, ultimately guiding us toward a more empowered existence. The Armadillo appears in Mesoamerican mythology, where it is often associated with the earth and the underworld. Its protective shell can symbolise the need for individuals to cultivate their inner resources and establish a strong foundation for emotional resilience.

In Mexican folklore, the Armadillo is depicted as a wise creature that knows when to shield itself and when to engage with the world. This embodies the dual nature of existence, balancing the need for connection with the necessity of self-preservation.

By respecting our limits and moving with care, we can navigate grief and life's difficulties with quiet strength and confidence

Fable | The Guardian of Boundaries
Armadillo wandered through the underbrush, its tough shell clinking softly as it moved. Nearby, Rabbit, curious and timid, watched Armadillo with wide eyes.

"Armadillo, why do you carry that heavy armour all the time?" Rabbit asked. "Doesn't it weigh you down?"

Armadillo turned and looked at Rabbit. "It's not just armour, Rabbit. It's my boundary. It keeps me safe from harm, letting others know where I end and the world begins." Rabbit twitched its nose. "But don't you ever feel trapped inside?"

Armadillo shook its head. "No, because I know when to lower my guard. Boundaries aren't about isolation. They're about protection. Without them, I'd be too vulnerable to the dangers around me." Rabbit nodded, still trembling slightly. "I wish I could have boundaries like that. I'm always so afraid."

Armadillo softened its voice. "Boundaries are built over time, Rabbit. They're not just about walls, they're about knowing when to open and when to close. Start small, and you'll find your way." The animals of the forest learned from Armadillo that boundaries are essential for self-protection, but they don't need to keep the world out completely. With balance and awareness, boundaries allow for both safety and connection.

The animals of the forest learned from Armadillo that strong boundaries are the first step to authentic growth. With protection comes freedom, and with awareness comes the courage to begin anew.

29
Badger

Self-expression (11)
Keeper of Stories

Badger's connection to the number 29 represents assertiveness and courage. It encourages you to be assertive in your healing, using your strength to push through the challenges of grief.

- **Opportunity:** Badger provides the strength to face grief head-on with tenacity, encouraging you to take action for your healing and to see beyond where you are right now.

- **Challenge:** The challenge is managing feelings of anger or frustration that can arise during grief, that may be borne from excessive worry.

Questions for today

Are you bottling up your anger or expressing it? How can you safely release pent-up emotions today? Are you feeling highly strung and need to be more grounded? What innovative ways can you find that help you connect to your path? How can you use your creativity and sensitivity to illuminate a path forward? What stories about yourself no longer serve you? What story would you like to create for your future self to be proud? How have you expressed yourself lately that has helped or hindered yourself and others? What part of your story needs to be heard?

Affirmation:
- "I channel my energy into positive and productive actions."
- "I am able to share my stories with more than my words."

Self-Care Activity

Practice relaxation techniques. Engage in deep breathing exercises or gentle stretching to help manage and release built-up tension. Try getting your hands in some soil, or gather leaves to crunch, these activities can help you address aggressive feelings in a healthy manner, while helping to ground those feelings. Write down your worries on a piece of paper and bury it somewhere.

Story

In many Indigenous cultures, Badger is honoured as a symbol of courage and assertiveness. It teaches the importance of standing firm in one's beliefs and emotions, showing that confronting challenges with strength is essential for personal growth. In shamanic traditions, Badger is associated with digging deep into the earth, symbolising the unearthing of hidden emotions and truths. This serves as a reminder that facing inner struggles, particularly during times of grief, can lead to transformation and healing.

Badger, the largest member of the weasel family, is also linked to the power of the spoken word. Its behaviour of digging and uncovering hidden things is symbolic of bringing truths to the surface, much like speaking one's story reveals emotions, lessons, and insights. Its presence encourages acknowledging and expressing our experiences, helping us process them and move forward. By embracing difficult emotions and persisting through challenges, we cultivate resilience and insight.

In European folklore, it is believed that Badgers can sense the unseen and are capable of guiding others through their emotional journeys, serving as a reminder to confront grief with tenacity. Through its example, Badger teaches that strength and careful reflection help us navigate grief with confidence and emerge transformed. The Badger encourages us to dig deep with courage to uncover and express hidden truths with insight and integrity.

Fable | Keeper of Stories
Badger burrowed deep into the earth, its claws moving steadily as it dug. Above ground, Squirrel sat on a tree branch, chattering excitedly about the coming winter. "Badger, you're always underground, always digging," Squirrel said. "What do you find down there?"

Badger poked its head out of the burrow, dirt clinging to its fur. "I find the stories of the earth, Squirrel. Every root, every stone, every layer of soil has a story to tell." Squirrel twitched its tail. "Stories? I thought you were just digging for food!"

Badger smiled knowingly. "Food is important, yes. But so are the stories. They connect us to the past, to those who came before us. Without them, we lose our way." Squirrel tilted its head. "But how do you share those stories when you're always underground?" Badger climbed out of the burrow and sat beside Squirrel. "I listen, and then I pass them on. Stories aren't always told with words, Squirrel. Sometimes they're passed through actions, through the way we live our lives. You can find the strength to assert yourself, in the courage to honour your truth."

The animals learned from Badger that stories are the threads that connect past and present. By listening to the earth and sharing its wisdom, they could learn the lessons of those who came before and carry those lessons forward into the future, letting go with no more need to worry the story will be lost.

30
Rabbit

Fear (3)
Overcoming Fear

Rabbit, aligned with the number 30, symbolises overcoming fear through creative expression. It teaches you to acknowledge your fears and face them with courage, allowing for growth and healing.

* **Opportunity:** Rabbit offers the opportunity to acknowledge your fears in grief, helping you confront them and move through them.
* **Challenge:** The challenge is overcoming the paralysis that fear can cause, allowing grief to flow rather than be blocked by anxiety.

Questions for today

How is fear showing up in your grief? What daily action can help you face and lessen your fears? What self-doubt are you perpetuating with your constant conversations about it? How can you better self-regulate your strong emotions and rely less on others for your healing and in doing so, how can you better communicate your story related to your loss?

Affirmation:
- "I face my fears with courage, resilience and creativity."
- "I am more than my fears."

Self-Care Activity

Practice grounding techniques. Engage in activities that ground you, such as walking barefoot on grass or practising deep breathing. These practices can help alleviate feelings of fear and anxiety. Stop for a moment and realise you don't need to talk about your fears to everyone, as this can simply build a belief that is not real.

In these pages, seek out the predator energy of the rabbit. Look at how they hunt the rabbit and seek to understand the qualities of this animal in supporting you in overcoming your fears. Use this energy to imagine the fear being consumed by the strengths and attributes of the predator.

Story

The Rabbit's teachings about fear and courage resonate deeply within the journey of healing from grief. By embodying both vulnerability and alertness, the Rabbit reminds us that acknowledging our fears is essential for growth. Through reflection, supportive connections, and small, courageous steps, we can face our anxieties, allowing grief to move rather than become paralysed by fear. Embracing our emotions in this way can transform fear into opportunities for personal growth and renewal.

Many Indigenous cultures view the Rabbit as a symbol of fear and transformation. They teach that confronting one's fears can reveal the courage needed to navigate life's challenges and emerge stronger. In the Chinese zodiac, the Rabbit represents peace, prosperity, and fertility, honoured in Spring as life and growth flourish. Ancient teachings also highlight the importance of awareness of one's surroundings while having the courage to take careful, considered risks. The Rabbit is also associated with creativity, adaptability, and the playful courage needed to navigate life's challenges with optimism and joy.

In Celtic folklore, Rabbits were considered sacred, often acting as messengers between the human world and the spirit realm. They symbolised transformation, hidden wisdom, and divination. While modern interpretations emphasise listening to instincts and using courage to overcome fear, these ideas are extrapolated from the Rabbit's broader symbolic role rather than directly documented in Celtic lore.

In grief recovery work, the Rabbit can also be seen as a representation of fear itself, while other animal energies serve as the strength used to confront and overcome it. This approach highlights the Rabbit's role in guiding us to face fear with courage, transforming vulnerability into insight and resilience.

Fable | Overcoming Fear

Rabbit darted nervously between the tall grass, always on edge, its ears twitching at every sound. Nearby, Deer grazed calmly, watching Rabbit's frantic movements with gentle eyes. "Why are you always so scared, Rabbit?" Deer asked softly. "There's no danger here."

Rabbit's eyes were wide, its body trembling. "But there could be, Deer. Danger is everywhere. I have to be ready to run at any moment." Deer lowered its head, its voice calm and reassuring. "Fear is natural, Rabbit. But if you let it control you, you'll never know peace. You don't have to run all the time. Sometimes, standing still and breathing is the bravest thing you can do."

Rabbit hesitated, its heart racing. "But what if something bad happens?" Deer smiled gently. "Then you face it, Rabbit. Fear is part of life, but it doesn't have to rule you. By facing your fears, you grow stronger."

Rabbit took a deep breath and, for the first time, stopped running. It stood still beside Deer, its heart still pounding but its mind beginning to calm. The animals learned from Rabbit that overcoming fear is a journey, and that sometimes the greatest courage lies in standing still and facing what frightens us most. Understanding your creativity and self-expression is hampered by fear can help you face those fears head-on, rather than running away.

31
Turkey

Sacrifice (4)
The Gift
of Sacrifice

Turkey's connection to the number 31 represents sacrifice, grounding and generosity. It encourages you to honour the sacrifices made in life, recognising the gifts they bring, even in grief.

* **Opportunity:** Turkey teaches that through sacrifice, whether it's letting go or releasing control, there is healing and transformation in grief.
* **Challenge:** The challenge is learning to release attachment to past experiences and the pain of loss, creating space for new growth.

Questions for today
What have you sacrificed during your grief process? How can you reclaim some of what you've given up to nourish yourself? Are you focused on keeping safe, rather than opening your mind to other possibilities for healing? Have you got caught up in being seen to do things for others' and forgetting the true purpose behind this? Have you become too grounded in the seriousness of life and all its challenges? Have you become anxious in daily life and need to refocus to gain stability and be more grounded?

Affirmation:
- "I honour the sacrifices made and find meaning in letting go."
- "I am grounded with the gifts of life with gratitude and humility."

Self-Care Activity
Engage in a giving activity of any description, one that makes you feel of service to others. Honouring your own needs is a way of sacrificing time for yourself and reinforcing self-care. Find a structured way in which you build a habit of giving that supports a greater sense of connectedness.

Story
In many Indigenous cultures, the Turkey is honoured as a symbol of self-sacrifice and generosity. Its teachings remind us of the importance of contributing to the wellbeing of others while maintaining personal integrity. Observing the Turkey encourages reflection on how our actions affect the wider community and inspires a sense of responsibility in nurturing those around us.

In American culture, Thanksgiving is a time to reflect on gratitude and the sacrifices made by those who came before. The Turkey's grounded presence and patient nature teach that true strength often lies in giving, serving, and supporting without expectation of reward. Its example encourages humility and perseverance while reminding us to balance personal needs with the care of others.

The Turkey reflects stability and discipline, reminding us that growth and resilience are cultivated through steady effort and a grounded approach to life. The Turkey serves as a central symbol, reminding people to honour the gifts that arise from hardship and loss.

Fable | The Gift of Sacrifice
The Turkey, with its symbolic role of sacrifice and generosity, taught the animals about the importance of giving and letting go for the greater good. It represented the concept of finding meaning and purpose through acts of sacrifice. Turkey walked slowly through the meadow, its feathers shimmering in the sunlight. Above, Eagle circled, watching from a distance.

"Turkey, you always seem so grounded," Eagle said, descending to perch on a nearby branch. "Why do you give so much of yourself to others?" Turkey lifted its head, gazing at Eagle with wise eyes. "Because in giving, I find my true strength. Sacrifice is not about loss, but about honouring the needs of others. It nourishes the community, and in turn, it nourishes me."

Eagle nodded thoughtfully. "But doesn't it make you weak?" Turkey shook its head gently. "No, Eagle. True power comes from selflessness. In sacrifice, we feed the earth and each other. What we give comes back to us in ways we cannot always see."

The animals learned from Turkey that sacrifice is a noble act, one that strengthens not only the individual but the entire community. Through giving, they understood that they were part of a larger whole, sustained by the balance of giving and receiving. Turkey showed that responsible, thoughtful actions create balance and build a strong foundation for healing and grief recovery.

32
Ant

Patience (5)

The Patience of Time

Ant, aligned with the number 32, symbolises patience, industriousness and teamwork. It teaches you to trust in the steady progress of healing, knowing that each small step matters.

* **Opportunity:** Ant reminds you that healing from grief is a journey, offering the opportunity to practice patience and endurance.

* **Challenge:** The challenge is resisting the urge to rush through grief, instead allowing it to unfold in its own time.

Questions for today
Are you being patient with yourself as you heal? What daily practice can help you slow down and trust the process? Have you been losing patience easily with others and regretting your words and actions? Have you been feeling rushed and frantic, almost to the point of burnout? Have you lost your discipline in basic everyday actions? Are you feeling stuck in the daily routines of life and feeling apathy towards all you do?

Affirmation:
- "I cultivate patience and trust in the process of healing."
- "I trust in the process and remain patient in my journey."

Self-Care Activity
Take a slow, mindful walk. Enjoy a walk at a relaxed pace, observing the details around you. This practice helps cultivate patience and mindfulness, allowing you to be present in the moment. Do a jigsaw puzzle, not rushing for completion to move to the next activity, but to enjoy the process towards completion.

Story
The Ant is a symbol of patience and hard work in various cultures. In many Native American traditions, Ants are seen as teachers of perseverance and diligence. They emphasise the importance of teamwork, showing how collaboration can lead to greater achievements.

In ancient Egypt, the Ant was associated with industriousness and the collective spirit of the community. It was believed that Ants possessed a special connection to the earth, teaching humans to work harmoniously with nature and one another.

Ants remind us that healing from grief is not a race but a journey of gradual progress. By embodying their patience and collective strength, we can learn to trust in the slow unfolding of our emotions and allow ourselves the grace to heal over time. The challenges we face in our grief can be met with the same tenacity and teamwork that ants exemplify, ultimately leading to a stronger, more resilient self.

Fable | The Patience of Time
The Ant worked tirelessly, gathering food and building its nest with incredible patience. During a long drought, the Ant's persistent efforts ensured that its colony had enough supplies to survive. The Ant's unwavering dedication and patience became a symbol of perseverance and the rewards that come from diligent and sustained effort.

The Ant, taught the animals that progress may be slow, but steady effort and patience lead to success and growth.

Ant marched diligently across the forest floor, carrying a grain of sand ten times its size. High above, Bear watched in awe. "Ant, why do you work so tirelessly, always moving, always building?" Bear asked.

Ant paused, looking up at Bear with unwavering focus. "Because patience builds the world, Bear. One grain, one step at a time, we build something greater than ourselves." Bear tilted its head. "But doesn't it take forever?"

Ant smiled. "Time is not something to fear. Patience is my greatest strength. It is slow change, but with discipline I have freedom in joy and my colony. What may seem slow to others is progress to me. In the end, the greatest achievements are not built in haste but with steady persistence."

Bear watched as Ant continued its journey, realising that true strength often lies in patience. The animals of the forest began to see that time, when respected and understood, could bring about lasting change. True patience is not passive; it is an active practice of persistence and adaptability, allowing us to navigate life's changes with steady resilience and purpose.

33
Weasel

Stealth (33)

The Master of Stealth

Weasel, connected to the master number 33, symbolises stealth, wisdom and healing. It is a Master Number focused on Unconditional Love for yourself. It teaches you to navigate grief with subtlety, using inner wisdom to guide your path.

* **Opportunity:** Weasel offers the opportunity to navigate grief with quiet strength and insight, observing and processing emotions without being overwhelmed.

* **Challenge:** The challenge is to avoid being overly secretive or detached, allowing yourself to express emotions openly when needed.

Questions for today
Are there parts of your grief you're avoiding? How can you gently bring these hidden feelings into the light? How are you connecting with your life goals through this process, while also showing leadership and humility in being of service to others? Have you got yourself into a tight spot you need to get out of carefully? Have you become too alone in your grief? Has someone assumed you are weak because you have been silent? Are you not trusting your own feelings about situations or people? Have you been too aggressive and hurt someone with your words?

Affirmation:
- "I move through my challenges with stealth and wisdom."
- "I honour my healing journey and connect with a higher consciousness."

Self-Care Activity
Practice introspective journaling. Spend time writing in a journal, focusing on your inner thoughts and feelings. This quiet, introspective activity allows you to reflect and gain insights away from external pressures. Consider who in your circle may need some indirect guidance and see how you may help them.

Story
In many cultures, Weasels are recognised as symbols of stealth and inner wisdom. Historically, they were valued in households for rodent control, and royalty often wore ermine fur, the winter coat of a weasel, as a sign of prestige and power due to its rarity.

The Weasel teaches that navigating grief can require quiet observation and careful discernment. By embracing the subtler aspects of ourselves, we can process emotions gently and authentically, learning to honour our experiences while cultivating patience and self-awareness. Its presence reminds us that healing often comes through attentiveness, subtlety, and the courage to explore hidden feelings. Through its example, the Weasel encourages us to approach grief with empathy and insight, transforming personal sorrow into opportunities for profound understanding and nurturing of both ourselves and others.

Fable | The Master of Stealth
Weasel moved silently through the forest, each step deliberate, each pause intentional. Grief had arrived like a shadow, confusing and heavy, and at times Weasel doubted its own feelings, telling itself it was fine or ignoring what it truly needed.

Its stealth allowed it to observe its surroundings and itself without distraction. By watching quietly, it noticed the subtle currents of its own emotions, the flicker of sadness it had been avoiding, and the truths it had tried to deny. In solitude, it learned to move through its grief without pressure, embracing each revelation gently and deliberately.

Often underestimated, Weasel's reclusive nature became a strength. Its intelligence and patience guided it through moments of uncertainty, teaching it to honour its needs without judgment. Each careful, hidden step allowed clarity to emerge, helping it distinguish between fleeting worries and the deep truths that required attention.

Through its mastery of observation and stealth, Weasel transformed doubt into insight. It learned that grief need not be a rush of loud expression, but a journey navigated with care and discernment. In its quiet vigilance, it reclaimed resilience and cultivated a sense of inner guidance, showing that profound healing can grow in silence, patience, and mindful attention.

Weasel smiled softly as it came to see that its stealth was not deception, but precision. Weasel moved with intent, understanding when to be seen and when to disappear. Stealth teaches us to navigate life with subtlety, to act when the time is right. It taught the animals the value of being discreet and strategic in their approach to obstacles and transitions.

34
Grouse

Doorway (7)
The Sacred Spiral of Life

Grouse, aligned with the number 34, symbolises the sacred spiral and life's cycles. It teaches you to embrace the natural rhythms of grief, understanding that it is part of the greater cycle of life.

* **Opportunity:** Grouse brings the opportunity to see the cyclical nature of life and grief, understanding that both are part of a greater, sacred journey.
* **Challenge:** The challenge is to release the linear perspective of healing, recognising that progress often moves in spirals.

Questions for today

How is your grief journey spiralling inward or outward? What small ritual can help you reconnect with your personal rhythm? How can you keep moving forward, while also exploring other avenues of healing such as writing, learning and researching new ways for yourself? What areas of the spiritual realm would you like to explore and learn more about? Are there ancient teachings that you are curious to learn more about that might open a doorway to understanding life's greater mysteries? What do you keep going around in circles with?

Affirmation:

- "I embrace the ongoing sacred movement of life and honour my journey."
- "I honour the doorway to understanding life's larger purpose."

Self-Care Activity

Engage in a meditative movement practice. Try yoga or Tai Chi to connect with your body and its movements in a mindful, circular way. Create or visit a labyrinth. This practice can help you align with the sacred spiral of life and renewal. Put some music on and have a dance in your home, or go out and dance like no one is watching! Try drumming, or listen to strong drumming and chants.

Story

In various cultures, the grouse is associated with sacred circles and cycles of life. Indigenous peoples of North America often viewed the grouse as a symbol of the Earth's cycles, representing the interconnectedness of all beings. Their dances, drumming and rituals incorporated the Grouse to honour the seasonal changes and the lessons embedded in each phase of life.

The sacred spiral is a powerful symbol of growth and evolution, reflecting the unfolding of life's patterns. It appears throughout nature, beautifully illustrated by the unfurling fern frond or a shell. It is often seen in ancient art in caves and on old pottery. It is seen as sacred geometry, indicating the journey of life that is not linear but spirals toward deeper understanding and enlightenment.

The Grouse teaches us that grief is not a linear journey but a sacred spiral, allowing us to delve deep into our emotions and experiences, and always moving forward. Through the Grouse's wisdom, we learn that every step, every spiral, brings us closer to understanding our place in the greater tapestry of life. In this way, we can embrace our journey with compassion and reverence, allowing the sacred spiral to guide us toward healing and growth.

Fable | The Sacred Spiral of Life
Grouse danced in circles beneath the great oak, its feathers fanned out in a brilliant display. Nearby, Mouse scurried in confusion, watching the graceful movements. "Grouse, why do you always dance in circles?" Mouse asked, tilting its head.

Grouse paused, its eyes glowing with ancient knowledge. "This is the dance of the sacred spiral, Mouse. Life is not a straight path, but a spiral of growth and renewal. Each turn brings us closer to our centre, and yet, we are always expanding." Mouse twitched its nose. "But doesn't it feel like you're going in circles?" Grouse chuckled softly. "Not at all. Every step I take brings me deeper into understanding. The spiral teaches us that growth is not linear. It moves in cycles, just like the seasons."

The animals learned from Grouse that life is a sacred dance, a spiral of experiences that guide them through the cycles of learning, growth, and renewal. Each step, though it may seem repetitive, brought them closer to their deeper selves.

35
Horse

Power (8)

The Power of Freedom

Horse, connected to the number 35, symbolises power and freedom. It encourages you to harness your inner strength, moving forward with determination and grace in your healing journey.

* **Opportunity:** Horse encourages you to reclaim your personal power and freedom in the face of grief, giving you the strength to move forward.
* **Challenge:** The challenge is to overcome feelings of helplessness and reclaim control over your emotions and healing journey.

Questions for today
How can you tap into your inner strength today? What habit can empower you to take charge of your healing? What can you do to create greater resilience in moving forward? What power do you need to take back? Have you tried to be too business-like in your healing? How can you find greater power and freedom in your responsibilities?

Affirmation:
- "I embrace my inner power and strength to overcome challenges."
- "I move forward with freedom."

Self-Care Activity
Exercise or engage in physical activity. Take part in a form of exercise that you enjoy, whether it's running, dancing, or hiking. This activity helps harness and express your inner power and strength. Go for a drive on a scenic route – use up some horsepower! Go horse riding.

Story
Horses symbolise strength, freedom, and the spirit of adventure. Their grace and power have made them central to human history, inspiring mythologies and spiritual teachings across cultures. They were often revered as companions for warriors and travellers, representing both physical strength and the ability to explore new territories. Observing the Horse encourages individuals to connect with their own inner strength and move forward with confidence and courage.

In many traditions, horses were considered sacred animals, bridging the earthly and spiritual realms. They appear in mythology as guides for Gods and heroes, highlighting the importance of recognising the spiritual dimensions of our journeys and the strength found in connection to something greater. Horses are also valued for their sensitivity to human emotions. Their gentle presence can facilitate healing, teaching patience, self-trust, and the understanding that recovery is a gradual process.

In ancient Greece, Poseidon, the God of the sea and earthquakes, was credited with creating the first horse. Horses were sacred to him, symbolising power and agility. The hippocampus (or hippokampos), a mythical creature with the upper body of a horse and the lower body of a fish or serpent, was linked to Poseidon and often served as the steeds for his chariot, representing his dominion over the oceans and appearing frequently in ancient art.

In Celtic and Gallo-Roman culture, Epona was the Goddess of horses, fertility, and protection, embodying the deep bond between humans and these animals and symbolising care and guidance. Her name, derived from the Celtic word for horse, highlights her central role as a protector of livestock and a patron of travellers, as well as a symbol of the deep human connection with these animals and the land.

In Welsh mythology, the Goddess Rhiannon is associated with horses and the moon; her magical horse symbolises freedom, transformation, and the cycles of life. The magical horses she rides symbolise freedom, transformation, and the cycles of life, particularly as she appears in *The Mabinogion*, a collection of medieval Welsh tales preserving mythology, folklore, and heroic legends. Rhiannon is seen as a counterpart to the horse Goddess Epona. Her association with fertility, rebirth, and the Otherworld highlights her strength and grace, emphasising her connection to both the living and the dead through her subtle, otherworldly magic.

Horses inspire strength, resilience, and freedom, reminding us that life's journey requires courage, perseverance, and trust in our own power and growth.

Fable | The Power of Freedom

The Horse was admired for its strength and vitality. During a great migration, the Horse led its herd across treacherous terrain, demonstrating its powerful endurance and determination. Its ability to harness and direct its power for the benefit of others established it as a symbol of strength and leadership, illustrating how power can be used to overcome challenges and support the community. The Horse, with its impressive strength and freedom, symbolised personal power and the ability to overcome obstacles. It taught the animals about the importance of embracing their own power and using it to navigate through challenges.

Horse galloped across the sunlit plains, each stride flowing with strength and grace. Its mane shimmered in the wind, a living symbol of vitality and freedom. A delicate Butterfly hovered nearby, wings catching the light. "Horse," it asked softly, "how do you move with such confidence and strength, aren't you afraid of losing control?"

Horse slowed, eyes meeting the Butterfly's. "Power comes from embracing your own freedom. Every step is intentional, and every movement honours who I am. True power is not about control, but trust. I trust in the strength of my legs, the wind that guides me, the earth beneath me and my path. Freedom is where my power is born."

The Butterfly fluttered closer, intrigued. "But sometimes the winds change, and the path is unclear. How do you stay steady?"

Horse lowered its head to the earth, breathing in the scent of the plains. "Steadiness comes from knowing your own rhythm. Life shifts, challenges appear, yet my power within remains. Freedom allows me to rise with each change, to move forward even when the direction is uncertain."

The Butterfly's wings caught the sun again. "So power and freedom are connected?"

Horse nodded. "Yes. When you honour your own strength and walk your path with purpose, you discover a freedom that cannot be taken away. Even loss or grief cannot diminish what you carry inside."

Grief, like the shifting winds, can guide growth and reveal the strength already within.

36
Lizard

Perception (9)
The Dreamer's Path

Lizard, aligned with the number 9, embodies intuition, transformation, and the wisdom that comes from completion. It invites you to pay attention to your dreams, as they may carry messages to guide your healing and personal growth. Through its quiet presence, Lizard encourages compassion for yourself and others and reminds you that letting go of what no longer serves you creates space for renewal and deeper understanding.

* **Opportunity:** Lizard teaches the importance of dreams in grief recovery, offering insights and subconscious healing.

✸ **Challenge:** The challenge is to avoid dismissing the wisdom that comes from dreams and your subconscious during grief.

Questions for today
Are you paying attention to your dreams during grief? How can you create space for imagination and reflection in your daily life? What is the perception you have of yourself in the past, present and future? Have you been giving away too much of yourself, or not open to receiving support? How have you been day dreaming about your life recently that is empowering?

Affirmation:
- "I honour my visions as guides on my healing journey."
- "I trust in my dreams and the wisdom they bring."

Self-Care Activity
Start a dream journal. Create a vision board. Spend time gathering images and words that represent your dreams and goals. This creative activity helps you focus on your aspirations and the possibilities for the future rather than just on events of the past. Spend time daydreaming of the life you would like to live, the person you truly want to be in this next chapter?

Story
In various cultures, Lizards are seen as symbols of dreams and intuition. Their ability to regenerate and their connection to the subconscious mind make them powerful teachers in navigating the complexities of life and grief. Their teachings encourage individuals to embrace their dreams, tap into their inner wisdom, navigate the complexities of grief with resilience and create their life with renewed

vision. By paying attention to the messages that arise from our dreams and trusting our instincts, we can embark on a journey of healing and transformation.

In Mayan culture, Kukulkan is a feathered serpent deity often associated with transformation and renewal. While not directly a Lizard, Kukulkan's imagery evokes the qualities of Lizards, symbolising change and the cyclical nature of life. The ancient wisdom associated with Lizards reminds us of the importance of embracing change. The Lizard is closely linked to dreaming and the subconscious, guiding individuals to explore hidden aspects of themselves. Its presence encourages reflection and self-awareness, reminding us that taking time to pause and observe can reveal insights that support personal growth and transformation. To let go of the past, you must also remain open to new possibilities as you navigate the path of grief.

Fable | The Dreamer's Path
Lizard lay stretched on a sun-warmed rock, eyes half-closed, feeling the pulse of the earth beneath it. It drifted in thought, exploring the possibilities that lived in the quiet spaces of its mind. Above, Eagle circled, wings cutting through the light. "Lizard," it called, "you spend so much time still. Why not move more, explore the world like I do?"

Lizard opened one eye, a gentle smile forming. "Eagle, I travel in a different way. I move through dreams, into a place where the future can be shaped. The forest, the river, the hills, they are not only what is, but what could be. In dreams, I see paths that the waking world cannot yet show." Eagle tilted its head. "But isn't dreaming just a form of escape?"

"No," Lizard said, stretching a claw toward the light. "Dreams are the blueprints of what we can create. In times of loss and grief, they guide us. They show what we need to heal, what we can build, and the hope we can carry forward. Without them, we wander without direction. With them, every small action takes us closer to something greater."

Lizard thought of the other animals it had inspired, of the forest thriving and the rivers flowing clear. "Dreams are also a mirror," it continued, "reflecting what we hold inside. They reveal doubts, fears, and truths we might hide from ourselves. Facing them, we find clarity and compassion to act."

Eagle landed softly on a branch nearby. "So, by dreaming, you are shaping not just the future, but yourself?"

"Yes," Lizard nodded. "By honouring dreams, we honour the self. Each vision sparks choices in the waking world. Grief teaches us to look inward, and dreams give us the courage to see what can come next, like compassion and forgiveness. Step by step, thought by thought, the future unfolds."

The animals of the desert learned from Lizard that grief and dreams are intertwined. By observing, reflecting, and imagining what is possible, they could navigate loss with hope, turning sorrow into a pathway for creation and growth.

37
Antelope

Action (1)
The Speed of Action

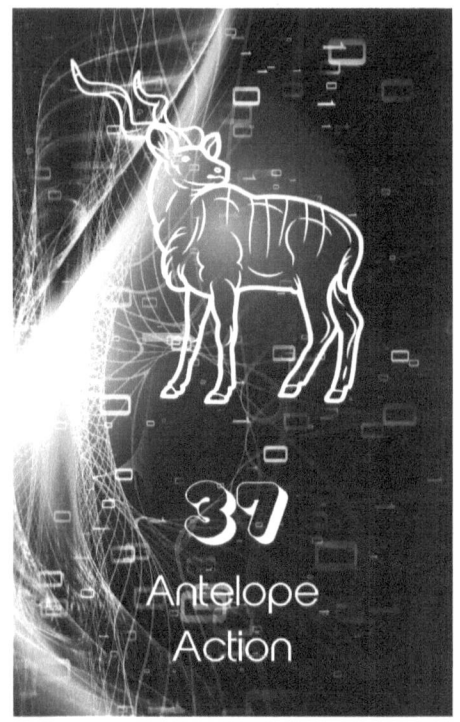

Antelope, aligned with the number 37, symbolises action and decisiveness. It teaches you to take active steps in your healing process, trusting in your own innate ability to move forward.

* **Opportunity:** Antelope encourages you to take decisive action towards healing, understanding that movement is essential in grief recovery.

* **Challenge:** The challenge is to overcome stagnation, doubt or hesitation in addressing your grief and taking the necessary steps forward.

Questions for today

Are you taking action to move forward in your grief, or feeling stuck? What one proactive step can you take today? How can you become more focused on yourself? What actions have you been putting off that you need to manage in your daily world? Are you not trusting yourself to help yourself or others? Are you using action and being busy as a distraction in healing with your grief?

Affirmation:

- "I take decisive action to move forward in my healing process."
- "I take action with originality towards my healing."

Self-Care Activity

Take a proactive step towards a goal. Identify a small action you can take towards a goal or project you're passionate about. Taking this step helps harness the Antelope's energy of swift action and momentum. Tackle that one thing you've been putting off – Antelope energy will help you make much needed progress.

Story

Antelope embodies action, decisiveness, and courage across cultures. Its presence encourages individuals to trust themselves and take steps forward in their healing journey. Observing the agility of the Antelope teaches us to navigate life's challenges with grace and to embrace personal growth and transformation.

In Native American traditions, Antelope is revered as a sacred animal and often seen as a messenger from the spirit world. Its swift movements and keen senses symbolise the importance of decisiveness and the ability to act with purpose. The Antelope's presence in various tribes' spiritual practices underscores its role in guiding individuals toward self-discovery and empowerment.

The wisdom of the Antelope reminds us that movement is essential for growth, showing that stepping boldly into life allows healing to unfold. Its swift movements encourage independence, self-reliance, and confidence, highlighting the importance of embracing one's own path and the power of taking action to shape life's journey.

Fable | The Speed of Action
The Antelope was swift and agile, known for its quick responses to danger. When a wildfire threatened the savannah, the Antelope led the animals to safety with rapid and decisive actions. Its ability to act quickly and effectively in emergencies earned it a reputation for courage and responsiveness, teaching the importance of taking decisive action when faced with challenges.

Antelope dashed across the meadow, its legs a blur of movement. Turtle, slow and steady, watched from the grass below. "Antelope, you're always running," Turtle said. "Why don't you ever slow down?"

Antelope paused, its chest heaving with excitement. "Because action is where life happens, Turtle. When the moment calls for it, I move. I don't hesitate." Turtle smiled gently. "But isn't there value in taking things slow, in thinking before you act?"

Antelope nodded. "Yes, there is. But there are times when speed is the key. When we hesitate, opportunities pass us by. Action requires trust in oneself and the knowledge that sometimes, we must move before we fully understand the path ahead."

Turtle, wise and deliberate, learned that there was a time for both patience and swift action.

38
Frog

Cleansing (11)
The Cleansing Song of Water

Frog, connected to the number 38, symbolises cleansing and renewal. It encourages you to purify your emotions and release any negativity, allowing for healing.

* **Opportunity:** Frog offers the chance to cleanse your emotional and mental state, releasing the heavy energy of grief.
* **Challenge:** The challenge is to face the emotional detox that comes with cleansing, allowing yourself to fully feel and release grief.

Questions for today

How can you cleanse yourself of the emotional weight of grief? What daily ritual can refresh your spirit? How can you be uplifted by sounds of rain, waves, brooks or streams? What pictures of water calm and soothe you? Are you drinking enough water to help clear your thoughts and what can you do to better calm your nerves? Do you need to take a soak or have a swim to feel better refreshed and connected to your body and soul?

Affirmation:
- "I cleanse and purify my emotions to support my healing."
- "I cleanse my spirit and release what no longer serves me."

Self-Care Activity

Take a cleansing bath or shower. Use your time in the bath or shower to release stress and cleanse both physically and mentally. Pop some lemon into a glass of water. This simple activity supports the Frog's theme of cleansing and renewal. Drink more water; make a nice cup of tea for yourself or to share with someone else. Map out your emotions if you are feeling overwhelmed.

Story

Frog embodies the qualities of transformation and adaptability. Their teachings inspire individuals to embrace change and find resilience in the face of grief. The ancient wisdom associated with Frog encourages us to recognise that healing is a journey of transformation, urging us to cleanse emotional wounds and embrace renewal. By learning from the Frog's ability to adapt and thrive in different environments, we can navigate our grief with grace. Ultimately, the lessons of Frog remind us that transformation is a natural part of life, encouraging us to trust the process and embrace the changes that come with healing.

Frogs undergo significant metamorphosis from tadpole to adult encouraging individuals to embrace the process of transformation, recognising that growth often comes from navigating difficult experiences. Frogs are primarily associated with water, which represents emotions, intuition, and the subconscious. By embracing and processing our emotions, we can facilitate healing and renewal.

In many cultures, Frogs are seen as symbols of cleansing and purification. Ancient teachings remind us that cleansing our emotional wounds through rituals or introspection can lead to renewal and a fresh start. They are also strongly associated with sound, especially when you can hear their 'ribet' after the rains.

Heket, the Egyptian Goddess of childbirth and fertility, is often depicted with the head of a Frog or as a Frog. She represents the transformative power of life and is associated with renewal. Her teachings encourage embracing transformation and the cycles of life, which align with the lessons of frog in navigating grief.

In various Native American tribes, Frog Woman is a revered figure associated with fertility, renewal, and the nurturing aspects of nature. Frog symbolises the importance of water and its role in life. Frog teachings highlight the significance of emotional connection and adaptability during times of change.

Fable | The Cleansing Song of Water

The Frog, with its connection to water, was known for its cleansing abilities. When the pond became polluted, the Frog used its natural instincts to clean the water and restore balance. Its role in purification and renewal established it as a symbol of cleansing and transformation, illustrating the importance of maintaining purity and rejuvenation in the environment and within oneself.

Frog sat at the edge of the pond, its throat bulging as it sang its evening song. Dragonfly hovered above the water, mesmerised by the sound. "Frog, your song is beautiful," Dragonfly said, landing on a nearby lily pad. "What does it mean?" Frog's eyes gleamed in the fading light. "It is the song of cleansing, Dragonfly. Water washes away the old, the stagnant, the heavy burdens we carry. My voice carries that cleansing power. It allows me to hear what I feel and what I need to release. When I call, I clear what is heavy inside, and the pond reflects it back, transforming it into something lighter."

Dragonfly tilted its head. "But can a song really cleanse?" Frog smiled. "Of course. Sound is as powerful as water. It moves through the air, through our bodies, clearing the way for new growth. Just as rain refreshes the earth, my song and the water refreshes the soul. The ripples in the water remind me of my own intuition. Grief can cloud the mind so I can see what is beneath the surface and become more attuned to my needs."

The animals of the forest began to gather near Frog's pond at twilight, listening to the cleansing song. They learned from Frog that renewal was not just physical, but emotional and spiritual, a cleansing of both body and mind.

39
Swan

Grace (3)
The Grace of Transformation

Swan, aligned with the number 39, symbolises grace and beauty. It teaches you to approach your grief with elegance and acceptance, finding peace within yourself.

* **Opportunity:** Swan offers the opportunity to embrace grace and beauty even in the midst of sorrow, transforming pain into elegance.
* **Challenge:** The challenge is maintaining composure and poise without suppressing your true emotions during grief.

Questions for today
Are you moving through your grief with grace? How can you embrace self-compassion in your daily habits? How can you better express your needs to others? Are you being overly pessimistic about life in general? Have you neglected your friendship groups and turned down invitations with disdain? How can you show more grace to yourself and those around you?

Affirmation:
- "I move through my healing journey with grace and ease."
- "I express myself through life with optimism and creativity."

Self-Care Activity
Practice gentle stretching or movement and connect with the earth. Engage in activities like stretching or a slow dance to move with grace and fluidity. This practice helps embody the grace and elegance of the Swan. Decide when and with whom you can show more grace to.

Story
Swan embodies the qualities of transformation, love, and inner wisdom. Their teachings inspire individuals to embrace their unique journeys, acknowledging the emotional depths associated with grief. The ancient wisdom associated with Swan encourages us to trust our intuition and seek beauty and harmony in our lives. Swan, connected to grace and beauty, carries profound symbolic meanings across various cultures.

The Swan's transformation from an awkward cygnet to a graceful adult reflects personal growth and the journey through grief. This metamorphosis teaches individuals to embrace their unique journey, recognising that beauty often emerges from struggles and challenges. Swans are often associated with water, representing the emotional depths and the subconscious. Ancient teachings emphasise the importance of connecting with and understanding one's emotions during grief, suggesting that acknowledging these feelings can lead to healing. Swans are known for forming lifelong pairs, symbolising deep love and loyalty. In many cultures, they represent unconditional love and emotional bonds, reminding individuals to cherish the relationships they have and the love that endures even after loss.

In Greek mythology, Apollo is often associated with the Swan, which symbolises beauty and harmony. The Swan's grace reflects the artistry of Apollo, encouraging individuals to seek beauty and harmony in their lives, even amidst grief.

Brigid, the Celtic Goddess acts as a symbol of hope and goddess of poetry, fertility, healing and craftsmanship and she is sometimes linked to Swans. Her teachings emphasise the importance of creativity and emotional expression, encouraging individuals to channel their grief into artistic endeavours as a means of healing. In Hindu culture, the Swan (*Hamsa*) is associated with the Goddess Saraswati, representing wisdom and purity.

The Swan embodies discernment, guiding us to seek clarity and truth in our grief. Its grace and dignity show how to move through life's transitions with poise and ease. From struggle, the Swan teaches that transformation and love can emerge, leading us toward healing and self-discovery.

Fable | The Grace of Transformation

The Swan glided gracefully across the lake, admired by all for its elegance. One day, a storm struck, and the Swan helped other animals find shelter with its serene and calming presence.

Swan glided effortlessly across the still lake, its reflection perfect in the water. From the shore, Otter watched.

"Swan, you move with such grace," Otter called out. "Swan, you move so beautifully. How do you make everything look so effortless?"

Swan turned its head slowly. "Grace comes from knowing yourself and letting your expression flow. When I move, I am sharing a part of my heart. Creativity is not only what you make, but how you move through life, how you bring meaning to each moment."

Otter twitched its whiskers, intrigued. "But isn't it hard to express yourself all the time?"

"Sometimes it is," Swan replied, dipping its wings lightly into the water. "But expression frees the spirit. It turns feelings into art, thoughts into movement, actions into love, and even sorrow into something beautiful. When we allow ourselves to create, we give shape to what is inside, and in doing so, we invite joy and connection."

The animals of the lake watched as Swan's reflection danced across the water. They learned that grace and creativity are intertwined, that beauty arises from embracing expression fully.

40
Dolphin

Breath (4)

The Song of Breath and Sound

Dolphin, aligned with the number 4, embodies joy, nourishment, and the stability that comes from intentional breath work. It encourages you to build routines of playfulness and connection, even amidst grief, as a way to strengthen your spirit and create a solid foundation for healing.

* **Opportunity:** Dolphin brings the opportunity to reconnect with joy and playfulness, finding healing in moments of lightness during grief.
* **Challenge:** The challenge is to not feel guilty for moments of joy or happiness that arise during the grieving process.

Questions for today
Are you nourishing your soul through your grief? What can you do today to bring more joy and energy into your life? Have you been working too hard and avoiding your feelings? Have you put too much structure in your life and not allowed any down time to explore your feelings and breathe?

Affirmation:
- "I receive and embrace the gifts of healing and joy."
- "I nourish my spirit with joy and playfulness."

Self-Care Activity
Try box breathing. Breathe in for 4 counts, hold for 4 counts, no breath for 4 counts then breathe in for 4 counts. This technique will help calm your parasympathetic nervous system in a minute or two and allow you to feel more energised, calm and ready to tackle challenges. Decide you will create an adventure for yourself, something daring and different that will help you tell a new story in the future.

Story
Dolphin carries the wisdom of joy, intelligence, and deep emotional connection, revered in many cultures as a bridge between worlds. Their playful leaps and flowing movements remind us that even during grief, moments of lightness can help us breathe again. Beneath their lively energy lies a quiet discipline, dolphins navigate vast oceans through intricate social bonds and finely tuned rhythms. This reflects a stabilising energy which builds safety and structure from within.

Dolphin teaches that healing is not found in endless motion or forced stillness, but in the steady patterns that hold us while we explore the unknown. In their way, they show that joy can be an anchor, not just a fleeting escape, a constant thread that steadies us as we move through sorrow and rebuild our sense of self.

Dolphins are highly intelligent creatures known for their sophisticated communication skills. This symbolises the importance of expressing emotions and communicating openly about grief, encouraging individuals to share their feelings with others to create healing.

Dolphins inhabit the ocean, representing the depths of the subconscious and spiritual realms. They teach us to explore our inner selves, connecting with our emotions and the spiritual aspects of healing. The ocean's vastness reflects the complexity of emotions experienced during grief. In various cultures, Dolphins are seen as protectors and guides. They are often believed to guide lost souls or provide protection during difficult times. This teaches individuals to seek support and guidance during their healing journey, recognising that they are not alone.

In Greek mythology, Poseidon, the God of the sea, is often associated with dolphins. These creatures are seen as messengers of the sea, symbolising harmony and guidance, and they encourage individuals to find balance and embrace the spiritual dimensions of life's challenges.

In many Polynesian and Pacific Island traditions, *manna* is understood as spiritual life force or sacred power that flows through all living things. It is not tied to dominance or control, but to the vital energy that comes from alignment with the natural world, integrity, and connection. Their playfulness and fluid movement are also said to awaken *manna* in the water, stirring life and vitality wherever they go. Ancient seafarers believed Dolphins carried blessings of protection and renewal, their joyful energy infusing the waters with vitality.

Dolphins are often seen as guardians of this life force, especially because of their relationship with breath. Unlike fish, they are mammals who must consciously come to the surface to breathe, which means every breath is intentional and aware. This act symbolises life lived with presence, each breath a reminder to return to the moment and honour the flow of energy within.

In Polynesian culture, Māui is a Demigod known for his adventures and cleverness. Dolphins are often depicted as companions to Māui, symbolising intelligence and playfulness. Their teachings encourage individuals to embrace creativity and resourcefulness in overcoming challenges. Many Native American tribes view dolphins as symbols of protection and harmony. They are often associated with the water element, representing emotions and intuition. The teachings from these cultures emphasise the importance of connecting with one's emotions and seeking harmony within oneself.

Fable | The Song of Breath and Sound
Dolphin darted through the waves, sunlight dancing across its back, moving with effortless joy. Nearby, Starfish called, "Why do you never stay still?"

Dolphin twirled in the water, letting a playful whistle escape. "Movement and breath keep me alive, Starfish. Each leap, each dive teaches me about the ocean—and myself. The patterns of currents, tides, and my breathing give me a foundation, helping me stay steady when waters are unpredictable."

Starfish hesitated. "But it feels chaotic…"

Dolphin circled gracefully. "It may seem so, but there is order in the play. Curiosity and rhythm sharpen the mind. Even in grief, the steady beat of breath and intentional movement keeps me grounded. Playfulness anchors me and turns uncertainty into clarity."

Starfish's eyes brightened. "So, joy and movement help you stay strong?"

"Yes," Dolphin said, surfacing for a deep breath. "Through exploration, play, and awareness, I honour myself and the world around me. Even in the deepest waters, I remain steady and resilient."

The reef learned that joy and curiosity are not frivolous, they are tools of resilience. Dolphin shows that consistency, care, and lightness of heart provide the foundation for navigating life's waves and emerging with clarity.

41
Whale

Creation (5)

The Ancient Song of Creation

Whale, aligned with the number 5, embodies freedom, adaptability, and the expansive flow of life. It encourages you to explore new perspectives and embrace change, using your intuition and inner wisdom to navigate uncharted waters. Through its deep song, Whale reminds you to honour the knowledge and experiences passed down through generations while remaining open to growth, adventure, and the transformative power of life's currents.

* **Opportunity:** Whale offers the gift of tapping into deep memories and emotional records, providing wisdom and perspective during grief.

❋ **Challenge:** The challenge is navigating the overwhelming emotional depth that remembering past events and loved ones can evoke in grief.

Questions for today

Are you reflecting on the stories of your life during grief? What memories can you revisit today to guide you forward? What memories are keeping you stuck? Are you seeking freedom from the past so you can create anew? Are you concerned people will feel that you have not spent enough time honouring your loss? What drama can you let go of now? What adventures are you not participating in for fear of not honouring the past? What family history would you like to explore and learn about?

Affirmation:

- "I honour the wisdom of the past and use it to guide my healing."
- "I access the knowledge of my ancestors and my inner wisdom."

Self-Care Activity

Start a journal where you can record your thoughts, memories, and experiences. This practice helps you keep track of your journey and insights, reflecting the Whale's role as a record-keeper. If your mind is too busy to hear your thoughts, find a way to clear them out through physical exertion.

Story

Whale embodies the qualities of wisdom, communication, and community. Their teachings inspire individuals to seek inner wisdom and express themselves openly during the grieving process. The ancient wisdom associated with whale encourages us to embrace our connections to nature and to each other, reminding us that collective support can lead to profound healing. Whales are often seen as ancient guardians of knowledge and wisdom due to their long lifespan and deep ocean habitat.

As creatures of the ocean, Whales are connected to the depths of the subconscious and the emotional realm. Whales are known for their complex songs, representing communication and expression. Whales often travel in pods, symbolising the importance of community and connection. This reminds us of the significance of support systems during grief, highlighting the value of shared experiences and collective healing.

In African and Afro-Caribbean Mythology, Yemaya is the Goddess of the sea and motherhood, often associated with Whales. She embodies nurturing, protection, and emotional healing, encouraging individuals to seek solace in their connections to nature and the nurturing aspects of life.

In Hindu mythology, the whale is symbolically represented through Matsya, the first avatar of Vishnu, who took the form of a giant fish or whale to save the sacred scriptures and the sage Manu from a great flood, preserving life and knowledge. This connects the whale to the cosmic ocean, or Kshira Sagara, which represents the source of creation and the vast, mysterious nature of the universe. Through this symbolism, the whale embodies preservation, protection, and the life-giving power of water.

In Hawaiian culture, whales, known as *koholā*, hold profound spiritual significance. The ancient Hawaiian creation chant, the *Kumulipo*, introduces the whale in its 16th verse, stating, *"Hanau kapalaoa noho i kai"* - *"Born is the whale living in the ocean"*. This highlights the whale's integral role in the cosmic order. Additionally, whales are revered as *'aumakua*, or ancestral guardians, believed to offer protection and guidance to specific families

Many Indigenous cultures have stories of Whales as spiritual beings that connect humans with the spirit world. These teachings highlight the importance of respecting nature and recognising the spiritual guidance available during times of loss.

Fable | The Ancient Song of Creation

The Whale, with its deep, resonant songs, was believed to hold the ancient knowledge of the ocean. When a great sea storm threatened the waters, the Whale used its songs to recall forgotten lore and guide the creatures to safety. Its role as the ocean's record-keeper established it as a symbol of wisdom and the preservation of knowledge, teaching the value of history and memory.

Whale swam slowly through the deep ocean, its massive body cutting through the water with ease. Above, Seagull flew, watching from the surface. "Whale, your presence is so powerful," Seagull called down. "What is the source of your strength?"

Whale's deep voice echoed through the ocean. "My strength comes from the ancient songs of creation, Seagull. I carry within me the memories of the earth, the wisdom of the oceans, and the knowledge of all that has come before." Seagull tilted its head. "But how do you remember all of that?"

Whale's eyes glowed with ancient knowledge. "Through the song of the Universe, Seagull. Every note, every sound is a thread in the web of creation. My song connects me to the past, the present, and the future. In each breath, I honour the story of all life." Seagull soared higher, realising the depth of Whale's wisdom.

Whales navigate vast oceans, moving effortlessly through shifting currents and vast expanses, symbolising the ability to adapt to life's uncertainties. Their deep, resonant songs mirror the rhythm of life, helping guide others through transitions and emotional shifts. The Whale embodies going with the flow, embracing transformation, and using emotional depth as a source of guidance and insight. Its presence encourages openness to change, resilience, adaptability and the courage to explore the unknown.

42
Bat

Rebirth (6)
The Harbinger of Rebirth

Bat, connected to the number 42, symbolises rebirth, nurturing and transformation. It encourages you to embrace the darkness as a necessary part of transformation, leading to new life and opportunities.

* **Opportunity:** Bat offers the opportunity for transformation and rebirth through grief, helping you emerge stronger and renewed.
* **Challenge:** The challenge is letting go of your old identity, embracing the transformative process that grief initiates.

Questions for today

What part of your life is ready for a rebirth through grief? What small change can symbolise new beginnings for you today? What nurturing activity can you do? Have you been avoiding going out at night? Have you lost sight of the path before you and need to envision a new version of yourself? Have you been playing the victim, forgetting that your power to create anew is within you?

Affirmation:

- "I embrace the process of rebirth and welcome new beginnings."
- "I acknowledge rebirth and transformation in my healing journey."

Self-Care Activity

Start a new habit. Introduce a small, positive nurturing habit into your routine that signifies a fresh start. This act of beginning anew aligns with the Bat's theme of rebirth and transformation.

Story

Bat embodies the qualities of rebirth, intuition, adaptability and community across various cultures. Their teachings inspire individuals to embrace transformation and trust their inner guidance during the grieving process. The ancient wisdom associated with Bat encourages us to confront our fears and seek support from those around us, reminding us that healing often arises from embracing change and navigating the unknown. Bat, symbolising rebirth, intuition, and adaptability, holds deep significance in various cultures, associated with the cycle of life and death, symbolising transformation and renewal.

Ancient teachings emphasise the importance of embracing change during grief, recognising that letting go can lead to new beginnings and growth. Bats rely on echolocation, representing the ability to navigate through darkness using intuition. This teaches individuals to trust their inner guidance during grief, encouraging them to explore their feelings and instincts as they navigate their healing journey.

Bats often live in colonies, symbolising the importance of social connections and support. Ancient wisdom reminds us of the value of community during times of loss, encouraging individuals to seek comfort and solidarity from those around them.

In Mayan culture, Camazotz is the Bat God associated with death and rebirth. He represents the transition between life and the afterlife, emphasising the importance of understanding the cyclical nature of existence and the potential for new beginnings after loss. In Chinese culture, bats symbolise good fortune and happiness. This comes from a wordplay: the Chinese word for bat (蝠, fú) is a homophone for the word for good fortune or blessing (福, fú). Such puns are a common method in Chinese art and decoration to create auspicious symbols.

Bats are creatures of the night, often representing the unknown aspects of life and the subconscious. This teaches us to confront our fears and uncertainties during grief, encouraging individuals to explore the deeper, often hidden emotions that accompany loss.

Fable | The Harbinger of Rebirth

The Bat, emerging from its cave each night, was known for its transformation from darkness to light. One day, it found a hidden cave where the spirits of past creatures dwelled. Bat flew silently through the night sky, its wings cutting through the darkness with ease. Moth fluttered nearby, drawn to the moonlight.

"Bat, you move so effortlessly in the dark," Moth said in awe. "How do you navigate the shadows?"

Bat circled Moth, its voice soft and steady. "Because, Moth, I have learned to embrace the darkness. In the shadows, I find my strength. Every time I sleep, I am reborn, emerging from the darkness with new insight and clarity." Moth hesitated. "But isn't the darkness scary?"

Bat smiled. "It can be, Moth. But darkness is also a place of transformation. Just as the night gives way to the dawn, we must sometimes journey through the shadows to find the light. Rebirth comes from embracing the unknown." The animals of the night began to see Bat in a new light, understanding that the darkness was not something to fear but a place of renewal.

From Bat, they learned that through the cycles of death and rebirth, they could find new strength and insight. Bat embodies nurturing and restorative energy, guiding us through the cycles of endings and new beginnings.

43
Spider

Creative Powers (7)
The Weaver of Fate

Spider, aligned with the number 43, symbolises creativity and intention. It teaches you to be mindful of the web you weave in your life, using creativity and intention to shape your future.

* **Opportunity:** Spider teaches that you are constantly weaving your own fate, offering the chance to create a new life after loss.
* **Challenge:** The challenge is accepting responsibility for the next steps in your life and not feeling trapped by grief.

Questions for today

How are you weaving together your grief story? What daily habit could help you make sense of your experience? How are your words impacting yourself and those around you? Have you felt disconnected from the world and believe you cannot control your fate? Is it time to reclaim the threads of your life and reconnect with people in your 'web'. Have you become forlorn and given up hope, only to believe this is now your fate?

Affirmation:
- "I weave the threads of my life into a tapestry of healing and growth."
- "I create my life with intention."

Self-Care Activity

Engage in a creative project. Take time to work on a craft or creative endeavour, such as knitting, painting, writing or bonsai! This activity reflects the Spider's weaving of connections and creativity. Reconnect with an old friend, or network or engage in your local community in some way. Write a card and send it via the post to someone you would like to thank.

Story

Spider, symbolising creativity, patience, and the weaving of connections, holds deep significance across many cultures. Its presence encourages individuals to explore their creativity, nurture relationships, and embrace the complexities of grief. Spiders remind us that life is an intricate web, where each action, word, or choice resonates through the broader tapestry of existence. A web unfolds naturally, reminding us that healing, too, follows its own rhythms and hidden patterns.

In Greek mythology, the weaver Arachne, renowned for her talent, challenged the goddess Athena and was transformed into a spider for her hubris. This story embodies themes of creativity, transformation, and the consequences of pride, serving as a cautionary tale about respecting one's abilities and the wider order of life. Similarly, Native American traditions honour 'Grandmother Spider' as a creator figure, teaching that all beings are interconnected and that relationships and choices ripple outward through the web of life. Hopi stories expand this symbolism, portraying Spider Woman's web as a reflection of destiny and guidance, where some threads are given and others shaped by human action.

Through these teachings, Spider encourages embracing shadows and the less comfortable aspects of grief, using creativity and mindfulness to navigate challenges. Its wisdom emphasises that strength emerges from patience, reflection, and deliberate effort, showing that even in the darkest corners, growth and insight can be woven into the pattern of life.

Fable | The Weaver of Fate
The Spider spun intricate webs, creating beautiful and functional designs that caught both food and light. When a great flood threatened the forest, the Spider used its webs to create bridges and shelters for the other animals. Its skill in weaving became a symbol of creativity and resourcefulness, illustrating the power of crafting solutions and connecting diverse elements.

Spider sat patiently in the centre of its web, its legs carefully tending to the delicate threads. Nearby, Cricket chirped, fascinated by the intricate design. "Spider, how do you create something so complex and beautiful?" Cricket asked.

Spider's many eyes gleamed as it responded. "I am the weaver of Fate, Cricket. Each thread is a choice, each connection a part of the greater tapestry of life. With patience and intention, I weave the web of my own destiny."

Cricket tilted its head. "But what if the web breaks?" Spider smiled knowingly. "Then I begin again. The web is a reflection of life itself, fragile, yet resilient. We are all connected in this web of existence. Through my weaving, I understand that even when things break, we have the power to rebuild."

Through Spider, the forest discovered the beauty of introspection and spiritual awareness. The web's rhythm, balance, and pattern showed that even in the unseen threads of life, there is guidance, hope, and a map to navigate challenges with understanding and grace.

44

Hummingbird

Joy (44)

The Joy of Lightness

Hummingbird, aligned with the master number 44, embodies joy, resilience, and the power to turn inspiration into action. It encourages you to notice the beauty in small, fleeting moments and to let these sparks of delight guide you in building a life grounded in purpose and meaning. Even amidst sorrow, Hummingbird shows that lightness, focus, and consistent attention to what nourishes the spirit can create enduring strength and bring dreams into form.

✳ **Opportunity:** Hummingbird invites you to rediscover joy and sweetness in life, even after experiencing deep grief.

* **Challenge:** The challenge is allowing yourself to feel joy without the guilt that often accompanies moments of happiness during grief.

Questions for today

Are you allowing moments of joy amidst your grief? What small act can bring a spark of happiness into your day? Does it make you feel happy to help others feel joy? What song, movie or book sweeps you away? Have you been feeling guilty when you laugh, realising that you are moving forward and worried you are letting go? Where in your daily routine can you pause to notice beauty or lightness? What creative expression can lift your spirit today? How can you turn a small inspiration into a meaningful action that nurtures you or others? Are you noticing and celebrating small achievements, even amidst sorrow? What tiny ritual or habit could ground you in joy and help you feel resilience in your heart?

Affirmation:

- "I embrace the joy and beauty in every moment of my healing journey."
- "I find joy and beauty in the smallest moments."

Self-Care Activity

Enjoy a moment of simple pleasure. Take a few minutes to indulge in something that brings you joy, such as a favourite treat or listening to uplifting music. Embrace the small joys that bring happiness.

Story

Hummingbird embodies the qualities of joy, love, and presence across various cultures. Ancient teachings encourage individuals to seek moments of joy and lightness in their lives, even amidst grief, as a way to honour their loved ones. Hummingbirds are drawn to flowers, symbolising the beauty of love and affection. This teaches us to cherish the love we have received and to express our feelings openly, allowing love to guide us through grief.

Hummingbirds are known for their ability to hover in place, representing the importance of being present. Ancient wisdom teaches us to focus on the here and now, embracing each moment as it comes during the healing process. They can also adapt to various environments and are known for their resilience. This encourages individuals to be flexible and open to change as they navigate their grief, understanding that healing can take many forms.

In Aztec mythology, the Hummingbird is associated with the Sun and rebirth. It symbolises the idea of life emerging from darkness, encouraging individuals to embrace the transformative power of grief and find new beginnings. Huitzilopochtli, the Aztec God of War and the Sun, is often associated with the Hummingbird. Huitzilopochtli's name derives from the Nahuatl word for Hummingbird, and he is frequently depicted as a hummingbird in Aztec art.

In different Native American traditions, the Hummingbird is seen as a symbol of love, happiness and beauty. They are considered to be messengers that carry good blessings. The Hummingbird teaches the importance of community and the power of love to transcend grief.

Fable | The Joy of Lightness

The Hummingbird flitted from flower to flower, spreading joy with its vibrant colours and cheerful humming. One day, the Hummingbird's energy uplifted a struggling garden, bringing it back to life with its joyful presence. The Hummingbird's role in spreading happiness and vitality established it as a symbol of joy and the importance of finding delight in the small moments of life.

Hummingbird flitted from flower to flower, its wings a blur of motion. Bee buzzed nearby, admiring the vibrant display. "Hummingbird," Bee said, "you move so quickly, always sparkling with energy. How do you carry such joy without tiring?"

Hummingbird paused in midair, its wings still beating rapidly. "Because I focus on the sweetness of life, Bee. I find joy in the small moments, in the nectar of each flower, and in the beauty that surrounds me."

Bee nodded thoughtfully. "But doesn't life get dark and heavy sometimes?" Hummingbird smiled. "Yes, but joy is what lifts us. By embracing the lightness of being, we can rise above the heaviness. Life is full of beauty if we choose to see it. Each beat of my wings is a choice to rise, to move forward, and to share that energy with others."

Hummingbird's joy was not just for itself, it flowed outward, connecting the garden in a subtle harmony, showing how attention and deliberate action can amplify energy beyond the self. Even in moments of heaviness, it demonstrated that by embracing lightness, movement, and focus, we can create ripples of vitality and renewal that touch everything around us, turning individual joy into a shared, enduring strength.

45
Blue Heron

Self-Reflection (9)

The Mirror of
Self-Reflection

Blue Heron, aligned with the number 9, embodies insight, awareness, and thoughtful reflection. Its patient, observant nature encourages you to step back and see your life and grief from a wider perspective. By reflecting deeply on your feelings, actions, and patterns, Blue Heron guides you to greater understanding of yourself and others, creating clarity, resilience, and compassionate self-awareness in your healing journey.

* **Opportunity:** Blue Heron offers the chance to deeply reflect on your grief and emotions, gaining self-awareness and insight.
* **Challenge:** The challenge is confronting difficult emotions and truths that arise during self-reflection in the grieving process.

Questions for today
Are you taking time to reflect on how grief is shaping you? What reflective practice can you incorporate daily? What personal challenges do you need to overcome? What are your true motives? How can you use these insights to develop yourself and improve your sense of certainty? Are you looking at yourself in a negative way, hoping others treat you differently? Now is a time to transform – can you feel that this is your opportunity?

Affirmation:
- "I reflect deeply and find clarity in my journey."
- "I look within to find my true self and purpose."

Self-Care Activity
Spend time near water. Visit a natural setting and take time to quietly observe and reflect. Being in nature can facilitate deep self-reflection and connection with your inner self. Consider how you may need to think more about the people around you right now and find ways to support them. This act of service is a profound act of self love.

Story
Blue Heron embodies the qualities of self-reliance, patience, and grace across various cultures. Their teachings inspire individuals to trust themselves and approach grief with dignity. The ancient wisdom associated with Blue Heron encourages us to embrace our independence and seek clarity as we navigate the complexities of healing. Blue Heron, symbolising self-reliance, patience, and grace, holds deep significance in various cultures. Known for their solitary nature, they also teach the value of self-reliance and independence in navigating grief.

Blue herons are patient hunters, often standing still for long periods. This teaches us the importance of patience in the healing process, encouraging individuals to take their time and observe their emotions without rushing to conclusions. Their graceful movements symbolise the beauty of navigating through life with elegance. This teaches us to approach our grief with grace, allowing ourselves to move through emotions while maintaining a sense of dignity.

In various Native American traditions, the Blue Heron symbolises self-determination and introspection. It teaches the value of patience and the importance of understanding one's emotions during the healing journey. The Heron's role in encouraging deep contemplation and understanding established it as a symbol of self-reflection and personal growth, teaching the value of looking within to find guidance.

Fable | The Mirror of Self-Reflection
The Blue Heron stood silently at the water's edge, its long legs steady, its gaze fixed on its reflection. In the quiet, it traced the ripples back to their source, learning to see beyond the surface. Nearby, Otter splashed curiously. "Heron, why do you stare so long at the water?"

Heron's voice was calm, measured. "The water is more than a mirror, Otter. It reflects who I am, my choices, and the possibilities ahead. By looking closely, I understand myself and the life I wish to shape." Otter tilted its head. "Isn't it hard to face yourself so directly?"

"Sometimes," Heron admitted. "But growth comes from honesty with ourselves. Reflection shows where we have stumbled, what we can change, how to move forward with clarity and love ourselves in the process."

The other animals observed, learning that stillness and contemplation reveal hidden truths. Through Blue Heron's example, they discovered the power of introspection, self-awareness, and the wisdom that comes from looking deeply within to guide their own paths. In embracing the lessons revealed through the water's mirror, the Heron embodies the wisdom and compassion of completion, learning from the past to move forward with clarity and purpose.

46
Raccoon

Dexterity (1)

The Master of Dexterity and Disguise

Raccoon, aligned with the number 46, symbolises protection, confidence and generosity. It encourages you to be a protector and nurturer for yourself and others, offering care and support during times of grief.

* **Opportunity:** Raccoon helps you protect your emotional boundaries while also offering care and support to others in times of grief.
* **Challenge:** The challenge is balancing self-protection with the need to offer and receive support from others.

Questions for today

Are you protecting your energy while grieving? What act of self-care can help safeguard your emotional well-being? Have you been shielding others from things they need to know? Have you been too generous in helping others? Do you need to speak up to ensure others are protected? Have you been masking your grief to help others feel better? What guilt and shame has created self-doubt? How are you pretending to be something you are not? What secret do you need to reveal to unburden yourself? What problem have you put off?

Affirmation:

- "I embrace the role of protector and offer my support generously."
- "I protect and nurture myself and others with generosity."

Self-Care Activity

Offer support to someone else. Reach out to a friend or family member and offer your help or a kind word. This act of generosity reflects the Raccoon's protective and caring nature. Find a way to give without expecting anything in return. Donate any old clothes, food or toys. Through being generous you will find the inner strength to let go of what no longer serves you, and heal.

Story

Raccoon, known for its cleverness, adaptability, and curiosity, holds a meaningful place in many Indigenous traditions of North America. Its behaviour teaches the value of observation and resourcefulness, showing that careful attention and ingenuity can help navigate challenges. The raccoon's dexterous hands and problem-solving skills symbolise the importance of using one's abilities thoughtfully and creatively, particularly in moments of uncertainty or change.

In Native American stories, the raccoon is often depicted as a trickster or teacher, demonstrating both the rewards and consequences of cleverness. These tales encourage reflection, patience, and adaptability, reminding individuals that insight often comes through experimentation, trial, and learning from mistakes. The raccoon's nocturnal nature also invites attentiveness to subtle signals and the unseen aspects of life, illustrating the need to balance curiosity with caution.

Through its example, raccoon guides us to approach life with wit and awareness, showing that challenges can be met with ingenuity and care. Its presence underscores the importance of adaptability and quiet observation, teaching that thoughtful actions, even small ones, can lead to meaningful growth and understanding. Raccoon also inspires initiative and self-reliance, encouraging individuals to take bold steps in shaping their own path.

Fable | The Master of Dexterity and Disguise
Raccoon crept through the forest under the cover of night, its nimble hands carefully unlocking a latch on a basket of fruit. Nearby, Owl watched silently from a branch. "Raccoon, why do you hide behind a mask and move in shadows?" Owl asked, curious.

Raccoon glanced up with a sly smile. "My mask is not to hide, but to adapt. In every situation, I find the tool I need to thrive. Whether it's disguise or dexterity, I use my skills to survive in this world." Owl blinked slowly. "But don't people misunderstand you for hiding your true self?"

Raccoon paused and nodded. "Yes, sometimes they do. But the truth is, we all wear masks. Mine helps me navigate the world with precision. Dexterity isn't just about my hands; it's about knowing when to reveal and when to withhold." Raccoon was known for stepping boldly where no one else dared to tread, trusting its own instincts when paths were uncertain. It carved its own way through the forest, proving that self-belief can light the way even in the dark. Its clever nature made it resourceful, able to turn obstacles into opportunities and find solutions where others saw none.

Owl considered this and flew off, realising that Raccoon's ability to adapt and hide in plain sight was not deception but a powerful survival skill.

47
Prairie Dog

Retreat (11)
The Wisdom of Retreat

Prairie Dog, aligned with the master number 11, embodies the power of retreat as a pathway to deeper insight. By stepping back from the noise of the world, you create space to listen to your intuition and access inner wisdom. This quiet withdrawal is not escape, but illumination, a way to tune in to the guidance that lies beneath grief's surface. Through stillness and introspection, Prairie Dog helps you reconnect with your inner voice and prepare to re-emerge with clarity and renewed strength.

❋ **Opportunity:** Prairie Dog teaches the value of retreating and resting to regain emotional clarity and strength during grief.

* **Challenge:** The challenge is avoiding prolonged isolation, ensuring that retreat does not turn into avoidance of healing.

Questions for today

Are you giving yourself permission to retreat and rest? What daily habit can help you create space for reflection and renewal? Have you disappeared from peoples lives and need to make an effort to rejoin your communities and networks? Have you been working too much to avoid your grief? Have you found little time to rest and unwind from life's daily grind?

Affirmation:

- "I honour the need to retreat and recharge for my well-being."
- "I find peace and renewal in moments of retreat."

Self-Care Activity

Create a personal retreat space. Set up a cozy corner with your favourite things where you can retreat for quiet time. Even better, go to bed earlier, or schedule in time for a nap, or a massage! This space provides a refuge for relaxation and rejuvenation. Take a weekend away, by yourself or with some friends. Book a retreat where you can truly focus on yourself and go within.

Story

Prairie dogs are small burrowing rodents native to North American grasslands, celebrated for their vigilance and strong community bonds. They live in large colonies known as "towns," with intricate tunnel systems that serve as homes, lookout posts, and escape routes, reflecting the importance of creating safe spaces for retreat and reflection. Their alert calls warn of danger, teaching us that stepping back and seeking refuge can be a vital strategy for protection and clarity, especially during times of grief.

Observing their daily routines - digging, foraging, and returning to burrows - highlights the value of pausing to process emotions and gain perspective. Prairie dogs show that retreat is not a sign of weakness but a necessary part of healing, allowing us to conserve emotional energy, reflect on our experiences, and prepare for renewed engagement with life.

Through their example, prairie dogs encourage us to honour periods of withdrawal and reflection during grief, trusting that these quiet, intentional pauses strengthen our awareness, resilience, and capacity to reconnect with others and move forward with clarity and purpose.

Fable | The Wisdom of Retreat

Across the wide, wind-swept plains, Prairie Dog lived quietly among her maze of deep burrows. While the other animals busied themselves on the surface, chasing the sun, she often slipped beneath the earth. "Why do you disappear?" they asked. Prairie Dog only blinked gently and said, "Because sometimes the heart grows too heavy for the open sky."

One evening, a hush fell over the plains when a beloved elder Buffalo passed away. The animals wandered aimlessly, each carrying their grief like stones. Prairie Dog retreated underground, not to escape, but to sit in stillness with the ache. In the quiet dark, she let the weight settle, listening to the soft beat of her own heart.

Days later, she rose from her burrow and found the others still scattered. With quiet steps and soft eyes, she guided them to sit beside her tunnels. "When grief is too loud," she whispered, "we must let silence hold us. Stillness is not surrender; it is how we hear our hearts again."

In her presence, the animals felt their pain soften. They realised her retreat had not been absence, but a sacred pause, a space where sorrow could breathe and where her quiet strength became a light for others.

From then on, whenever grief touched the plains, the animals followed Prairie Dog's example: they allowed themselves to retreat, trusting that in stillness, the heart remembers how to rise, and in silence, even the deepest pain can be carried together.

48
Wild Boar

Confrontation (3)
The Courage of Confrontation

Wild Boar, aligned with the number 48, symbolises confrontation and bravery. It teaches you to face your grief head-on, with courage and determination, rather than avoiding it. Grief often brings overwhelming emotions, but by facing them directly, rather than avoiding them, you can begin to heal and move forward.

* **Opportunity:** Wild Boar encourages you to confront the emotions you've been avoiding, allowing for transformation through grief.
* **Challenge:** The challenge is overcoming the fear of facing difficult emotions head-on.

Questions for today
Are you confronting your grief, or avoiding it? How can you gently face your emotions head-on today? Have you neglected a part of yourself that you used to love and enjoy expressing? How can you find the courage to move forward and express your emotions in the way you need to? Who, or what, needs to be confronted in your life?

Affirmation:
- "I face my challenges head-on with strength and courage."
- "I embrace my challenges with courage and determination."

Self-Care Activity
Address a small challenge directly. Tackle a minor issue or task you've been avoiding. Confronting it with courage helps build resilience and mirrors the Wild Boar's strength in facing challenges. Sit quietly and think about things you have been avoiding and work through a plan to allow you to get on with it before it becomes an issue.

Story
Wild boars are fearless creatures that protect their young. This teaches the importance of courage in navigating emotional pain and standing up for oneself during times of difficulty. As foragers, wild boars are closely connected to the earth, symbolising the importance of grounding oneself during emotional upheaval. This encourages individuals to stay connected to nature and their physical bodies as a way to find stability. Wild boars confront threats head-on, teaching us to face our fears rather than avoid them. This empowers individuals to confront the emotions associated with grief and take proactive steps toward healing.

Wild Boar embodies the qualities of strength, courage, and groundedness across various cultures. Their teachings inspire individuals to draw on their inner strength, confront fears, and embrace grit and resilience during the grieving process.

Freyr, the Norse God of fertility and prosperity, is sometimes depicted with a wild magical golden boar named Gullinbursti. This connection symbolises abundance and the strength to overcome challenges. In Roman mythology, Diana, the Goddess of the hunt, is often associated with wild boars and was sometimes a patron for those living outside society's constraints. In Celtic mythology, the wild boar is revered for its strength and bravery. It teaches the importance of resilience and the ability to confront challenges with courage.

The ancient wisdom associated with wild boar encourages us to stand firm in the face of adversity and to honour our personal power. Wild boars are known for their physical strength and determination, teaching us that drawing on inner strength can help individuals face the challenges of grief head-on.

Fable | The Courage of Confrontation

Deep in the forest, Wild Boar thundered through the undergrowth, scattering leaves in its wake. A fallen tree blocked the narrow path, its roots tangled like old fears. From a low branch, Magpie tilted its head. "Boar, you always charge at what stands before you. Aren't you afraid of breaking yourself?"

Wild Boar pawed the earth and met Magpie's gaze. "Fear visits, yes. But I move through it. Each obstacle is a canvas, and my courage carves the way forward. If I stop, the path stays closed. If I push, I create something new."

Magpie fluttered closer, intrigued. "Create? From struggle?"

Boar pressed its tusks against the bark until it cracked, opening a new gap in the forest floor. "When we face what blocks us, we break the old shape of things. We open space for new growth, for new voices, for new ways to be."

The animals later walked through the path Boar had cleared, feeling something shift inside themselves. They saw that courage was not only strength, it was the spark that transforms fear into movement, pain into power, and silence into expression. From Wild Boar they learned that facing life head-on is how we shape the world, and how we reshape ourselves. The Wild Boar, with its bold and fearless nature, symbolised the power of confronting challenges directly. It taught the animals about the importance of facing difficulties with strength and courage, rather than avoiding them.

49
Salmon

Wisdom (4)
The Wisdom of
Inner Knowing

Salmon, aligned with the number 4, symbolises steadfast wisdom and trust in life's currents. Guided by an instinct that leads it home, Salmon shows the power of perseverance and inner knowing. Its upstream journey reflects the discipline and steady strength needed to navigate hardship. In grief, Salmon reminds you to trust your path, draw on hard-won wisdom, and keep moving with quiet determination, building stability as you go.

* **Opportunity:** Salmon represents the wisdom gained through life's challenges, offering the chance to access deep insight and understanding in the midst of grief.

✽ **Challenge:** The challenge is trusting the flow of life, even when it feels like you are swimming upstream against adversity and loss.

Questions for today

What wisdom has your grief journey revealed to you? How can you integrate that wisdom into your daily routine? Have you ignored your gut feelings only to be proven right later on? What are you working so hard to avoid? Where in your life can you apply steady, practical effort to support your healing? Are there patterns or instincts guiding you that you've overlooked? What foundations are you building now that will support you in the long term? How can you create structure or rituals that honour what you've learned through loss? When have you felt an inner pull to keep going, even when the path was difficult? What "home" or inner truth are you instinctively swimming back toward? Where might discipline and consistency give you a sense of stability right now? What lessons keep resurfacing, asking to be acknowledged?

Affirmation:
- "I draw on my inner wisdom to guide my healing journey."
- "I trust the wisdom of my journey and embrace the lessons it brings."

Self-Care Activity

Spend time contemplating the lessons you've learned from past experiences. Write the first things that come to mind without hesitating. Writing or meditating on these can help integrate the wisdom you've gained. Think and discuss with a friend about any advice you have been given that you've ignored – find a way to tap back into that with an open mind and heart.

Story

Salmon embodies determination, intuitive strength, and the wisdom gained through lived experience. Across cultures, its journey upstream reflects resilience and a deep trust in inner guidance. Salmon's unwavering instinct to return to its source reminds us to rely on our inner compass when life becomes turbulent.

Ancient teachings honour Salmon as a guide through life's natural cycles. Its upstream journey symbolises the steady perseverance needed to overcome obstacles, encouraging us to move forward with discipline and quiet strength. Through this, Salmon shows that healing often comes from trusting our path and building a stable inner foundation that holds firm, even in powerful currents.

Many Indigenous cultures, particularly on the Pacific Northwest Coast and in Alaska, view salmon as a central, sacred part of their existence, with figures and stories like Salmon Woman, a powerful figure associated with the abundance of salmon and the cycles of life. Her teachings emphasise the importance of respecting nature and the interconnectedness of all living beings. Ishkur, the God of Storms and Rain in Mesopotamian Mythology, is associated with rivers and the life they support. This connection highlights the importance of water in sustaining life and emotional healing.

In Celtic mythology, the salmon represents wisdom and knowledge. The story of the Salmon of Knowledge teaches the importance of seeking wisdom from experiences and the depths of our emotions.

Salmon have an innate ability to navigate their environment, teaching the value of trusting one's intuition. Ancient wisdom encourages individuals to listen to their inner voice during times of grief. The life cycle of salmon represents the natural cycles of life and death. This teaches individuals to embrace the ebb and flow of emotions, recognising that grief is part of the greater cycle of existence.

As creatures of water, salmon symbolise emotions and intuition, emphasising the importance of connecting with one's emotional depths and using water as a source of healing.

Fable | The Wisdom of Inner Knowing
Once upon a time, rivers wound like silver threads through the forest, their currents shifting with the seasons. Young Salmon played in gentle waters, darting through pools touched by light. One day, a quiet call rose within her, pulling her toward distant headwaters where her ancestors had swum. The journey would be long and uncertain, yet the pull was as sure as her heartbeat.

She began her ascent, meeting rapids and falls that tested every fibre of her being. With each obstacle, she learned to pace herself and trust the rhythm within. Step by step, she built an inner structure strong enough to hold her steady when the current surged against her.

Wolf watched from a mossy bank, curious. "Salmon, how do you know where to go when the river twists?" Salmon rose in a shimmer of spray. "Because the path is within me. The river changes, but my foundation remains. Each trial has made it stronger. That is how I endure."

When she reached the sacred headwaters, her spirit was steady, shaped by the journey as much as by the water. The animals saw that her strength lay not only in reaching her goal, but in the inner framework she built along the way. Salmon showed that wisdom grows through discipline and quiet determination, turning even wild waters into a path home.

50
Alligator

Initiation and Integration (5)
The Power of Integration

Alligator, aligned with the number 5, embodies adaptability, awareness, and personal growth. It encourages you to face your grief directly, observing your emotions and experiences without judgement. Through its patient and watchful presence, Alligator teaches how to bring together memories and feelings into a balanced understanding of yourself. Grief can scatter the heart, but embracing each part of your experience builds resilience and insight. Alligator reminds us that transformation comes from fully engaging with life and allowing change to guide growth.

✻ **Opportunity:** Alligator offers the chance to integrate all parts of your grief experience, allowing you to process emotions in a balanced and grounded way.

* **Challenge:** The challenge is to resist the urge to compartmentalise emotions, ensuring that you face and process all aspects of your grief fully.

Questions for today
Are you integrating all aspects of your grief? What can you do today to acknowledge and balance your emotional experiences? Have you been trying to do too many healing practices to the point they have become a distraction from actual healing? Is it now time to integrate that knowledge into action for your grief recovery process? What do you need to initiate in your life to help you move forward?

Affirmation:
- "I integrate my experiences and find balance within myself."
- "I initiate change in my life."

Self-Care Activity
Practice mindfulness. Engage in mindfulness exercises to bring together your thoughts and feelings into a cohesive whole. This practice supports the Alligator's theme of integration and balance. Write down a list of all your achievements, those that hold real meaning to you. They can be very personal to you, there is no need for them to be externally recognised achievements. Recognising this can bring this into the whole of your being and support your next move.

Story
Alligator embodies the qualities of primal strength, patience, and integration. Its presence teaches us to bring together instinct,

awareness, and emotion, showing that true healing comes from uniting all aspects of ourselves. By observing how an alligator balances stillness with decisive action, we learn to integrate our grief and life experiences, transforming challenges into wisdom and resilience.

In Native American traditions, especially among Southeastern tribes like the Seminole, Choctaw, and Creek, alligators are powerful river and swamp guardians. They symbolise survival, adaptability, and the ability to move between land and water. This dual nature reflects the process of integration, connecting emotional depth with grounded action, and encourages individuals to flow with life while remaining anchored during times of change.

Alligators' patience and precise timing highlight the value of deliberate action after reflection, a lesson in harmonising inner and outer worlds. Their connection to water emphasises emotional depth, while their terrestrial presence reminds us to remain practical and centred. This balance embodies the adventurous, dynamic energy, encouraging curiosity, adaptability, and embracing life's transformations as opportunities to grow.

Fable| The Power of Integration
In the ancient swamps, Alligator was known for her patience and keen awareness. She watched the world from beneath the water's surface, seeing both the light and shadows above. One day, the creatures of the swamp were divided by a great storm, their homes and lives scattered. They looked to Alligator for guidance. Instead of rushing, she slowly surfaced, bringing together the elements of both water and land, teaching the creatures how to blend their experiences into one harmonious whole. Through this act, Alligator showed that the key to surviving hardship was not to separate parts of oneself but to integrate them into a stronger, unified being.

Alligator lay motionless in the swamp, only its eyes visible above the water. Nearby, Frog hopped on a lily pad, watching cautiously.

"Alligator, you seem so still and patient. What are you waiting for?" Frog asked. Alligator's eyes glimmered as it slowly blinked. "I am not waiting, Frog. I am integrating. I take in the lessons of my surroundings, the movements of the water, the whispers of the wind, and when the time is right, I act." Frog croaked curiously. "But doesn't that take a long time?"

Alligator grinned. "Yes, but patience is the key to true integration. To act without fully understanding is to waste energy. I move when I have gathered all the knowledge I need, and then, my actions are powerful and precise." The animals soon realised that Alligator's stillness was not laziness but wisdom.

From Alligator, they learned that by integrating their experiences and observations, they could act with greater strength and clarity. The Alligator, with its powerful presence and connection to both land and water, symbolised the process of integration and finding balance. It taught the animals about the importance of harmonising different aspects of their lives for overall well-being.

51
Jaguar

Integrity (6)
The Integrity of Impeccability

Jaguar, aligned with the number 6, embodies responsibility, harmony, and ethical strength. It encourages you to honour your truth and act in alignment with your values, even in the face of grief. By staying accountable to yourself and nurturing balance in your life and relationships, you cultivate resilience and clarity. Jaguar shows that integrity is not just moral courage - it is the disciplined practice of living authentically, caring for yourself and others, and creating harmony through every decision.

✻ **Opportunity:** Jaguar offers the opportunity to confront your shadows, facing the fears, regrets, or suppressed emotions that grief can stir up.

* **Challenge:** The challenge is to embrace the darker, hidden aspects of grief without letting them consume or overwhelm you.

Questions for today

Are you honouring your truth as you move through grief? What daily action can help you stay true to yourself? What people are challenging you to find greater alignment with your own path and healing? What aspects of yourself have you let go to make others happy? What parts of yourself do you need to reclaim and heal? Have you allowed jealousy to cloud your judgement? Have you been asked to act against your values?

Affirmation:

- "I embrace my personal integrity and stay true to myself."
- "I live aligned to my values in all aspects of my life."

Self-Care Activity

Align your actions with your values. Take time to reflect on your core values and ensure your actions are consistent with them. Feel empowered to change activities that no longer serve you through this journey. This practice reinforces your integrity and authenticity.

Story

Jaguar embodies the qualities of power, intuition, and the balance between life and death across various cultures. Their teachings inspire individuals to embrace their strength, trust their instincts, and seek spiritual support during the grieving process. The ancient wisdom associated with jaguar encourages us to navigate the depths of our emotions with courage and resilience. Jaguar, symbolising power, intuition, and the balance between life and death, holds deep significance in various cultures.

Jaguars are apex predators, representing power and dominance in their environment. They teach individuals to embrace their inner strength and assertiveness, particularly in times of grief.

In Mesoamerican traditions, the Maya revered the Jaguar as Balam, a guardian of the night and the underworld, guiding souls and connecting the living with their ancestors. The Aztecs linked the jaguar with warriors, strength, and courage, celebrating its role in confronting fear and uncertainty.

In the Andean regions, the jaguar was seen as a protector of the earth, symbolising harmony with nature and offering spiritual insight to those who sought its guidance. Among Amazonian tribes, it was considered a spirit guide and healer, teaching resilience, self-assertion, and the ability to perceive hidden truths.

Across these cultures, the Jaguar's qualities, stealth, observation, and disciplined power, illustrate that true strength is not merely physical, but also moral and intuitive. For those navigating grief or transformative experiences, the Jaguar reminds us to trust our instincts, face our fears, and move through challenges with integrity, courage, and inner wisdom.

Fable | The Integrity of Impeccability

Jaguar padded silently through the dense jungle, its golden eyes sharp and focused. Nearby, Parrot squawked loudly from a branch, observing the sleek predator. "Jaguar, you move with such purpose. How do you stay so impeccable in everything you do?" Parrot asked. Jaguar paused beneath the tree, its gaze unwavering. "Because,

Parrot, I live with integrity. Every step I take is intentional, every action aligned with my purpose. To be impeccable is to live in harmony with one's true nature." Parrot ruffled its feathers. "But what if you make a mistake?"

Jaguar's tail swished slowly. "Mistakes happen, Parrot. But living with integrity means acknowledging them, learning from them, and not straying from the path. Impeccability is not about perfection—it's about staying true to oneself in every action, no matter the outcome." The animals of the jungle admired Jaguar's grace and strength, learning that to live impeccably was to live with honesty and purpose. From Jaguar, they understood that integrity was the foundation of true power.

52
Black Panther

Mystery (7)

Embracing the Mystery of the Unknown

Black Panther, aligned with the number 52, symbolises the mystery and power of the unknown. It encourages you to trust in the mysteries of life and death, knowing that not all answers are immediately clear, but that there is wisdom in embracing the unknown. Grief often feels like a journey through the unknown, but trusting in the mystery of life and death can lead you to growth and understanding, even when the path is unclear.

* **Opportunity:** Black Panther helps you embrace the mystery of the unknown in grief, encouraging you to trust the unseen forces at work in your healing journey.

* **Challenge:** The challenge is overcoming the fear of the unknown

and learning to trust the process of healing, even when the future feels uncertain.

Questions for today

Are you open to the mysteries that grief brings? How can you embrace the unknown and find trust in your healing process today? What can you learn by sitting quietly with your thoughts and feelings? Is it time to reach out to someone for help? Is it time to explore your intuition or inner guidance for insight? Where in your grief might letting go of certainty open space for understanding? How can reflection or meditation help you notice patterns or truths you've overlooked? Is there someone you can reach out to who might offer perspective or support? What questions do you need to hold in patience rather than immediately seek answers for?

Affirmation:
- "I acknowledge the mystery of endings and find strength in uncovering what I need to know."
- "I embrace the mystery of life and trust in the unknown."

Self-Care Activity

Embrace a night outside. Spend time in a peaceful setting, reflecting on the mysteries and uncertainties in your life. This practice helps you find comfort and strength in the unknown. Use a star gazing app or telescope to look beyond our skies.

Story

Black Panther embodies power, mystery, and protection. Its presence encourages individuals to explore the unseen aspects of life, face hidden fears with courage, and trust their intuition while navigating emotional challenges. In the context of grief, the Black Panther teaches that healing often requires moving through shadowed or unknown spaces, observing carefully, and cultivating inner wisdom.

In many Native American traditions, the Black Panther is regarded as a guardian of sacred and spiritual realms, representing protection and the courage to confront what is hidden. Its dark, elusive nature symbolises the mystery of life and the unseen forces that guide and protect us. The panther's ability to move silently through hidden spaces inspires trust in one's instincts and awareness of subtle energies.

By observing and learning from the Black Panther, individuals are reminded that introspection, discernment, and spiritual insight are essential for transformation. Known for their stealth, strength, and connection to the shadows, Black Panthers teach the importance of creating emotional boundaries while exploring the depths of the subconscious.

Fable | Embracing the Mystery of the Unknown

In the velvety darkness of night, Black Panther roamed the forest with quiet elegance. She was a creature of mystery, her path always hidden, yet her steps sure and graceful. The other animals often asked her, "How do you navigate when there is no light?" Panther would smile and say, "The night holds many answers, but only for those willing to walk in the shadows."

Black Panther slinked through the shadows of the dense forest, its black coat blending seamlessly with the night. Rabbit, cautious and curious, peered out from behind a bush. "Panther, why do you thrive in the darkness?" Rabbit asked softly. "Doesn't the unknown frighten you?"

Panther's eyes gleamed in the moonlight as it smiled. "The unknown is where true power lies, Rabbit. In the mystery, I find my strength.

Fear comes from what we don't understand, but when we embrace the unknown, we uncover its beauty and potential."

Rabbit twitched its ears nervously. "But isn't it dangerous?" Panther nodded slowly. "Yes, it can be. But danger is part of life. By stepping into the mystery, we learn to navigate fear and uncertainty with grace. The unknown is not something to fear but something to explore." The animals of the forest learned from Black Panther that by embracing the unknown, they could move beyond fear and discover new possibilities. Panther's journey through the darkness became a lesson in courage and trust.

53
Lioness/ Lion

Feminine Power (8)

The Power of Feminine Assertion

Aligned with the number 53, Lioness symbolises the power and assertion of the feminine energy. In grief, this energy teaches us to lead with courage, nurture ourselves, and assert our needs as we navigate loss. Just as the lioness protects and leads her pride with strength and grace, you too can harness the power of the feminine to assert yourself during times of vulnerability.

* **Opportunity:** Lioness helps you assert yourself in the grief process by embracing your inner strength and feminine wisdom, showing you how to lead with grace, even in your pain.

✱ **Challenge:** The challenge is to balance nurturing your emotions while asserting your needs and boundaries in the face of loss.

Questions for today

How can you assert your needs in this grief process without losing touch with your softer, nurturing side? What power do you need to reclaim? Have you lost your sense of ambition? Do you need to set new goals and be more strategic about that? Have you become ruthless or overly competitive? Are you working too much and neglecting your home life – your own 'pride'? Are you finding it hard to let go of control? When can you be more practical and efficient in handling your resources?

Affirmation:

- "I lead with strength and grace, embracing the power of the feminine in my healing."
- "I assert my needs with compassion and stand strong in my journey."

Self-Care Activity

Write down the boundaries you need to create during your healing process. Assert these boundaries with kindness and honour your emotional needs. Surround yourself with people who respect and encourage your voice and contributions. Light candles, journal, or create a small altar to acknowledge your personal power and achievements.

Story

The Lioness inspires individuals to embrace their strength and take charge of their healing journey. While the male lion represents authority and protection, the lioness demonstrates the power of feminine assertion through focused action and nurturing, showing that her leadership blends insight, courage, and care.

Lionesses work together to raise their young and protect their pride, highlighting the importance of community support during times of grief. Their example encourages healthy emotional expression, finding balance between strength and gentleness, and leaning on loved ones while offering support in return. Sekhmet, the lion-headed Egyptian Goddess, symbolises power, protection, and healing. Her teachings emphasise the importance of embracing one's strength and using it wisely during the healing process.

Feminine energy cannot exist without the balance of masculine energy. Lions are known as the kings of the jungle, representing courage and strength. They teach individuals to embrace their power and face challenges head-on, especially during times of grief. Leading their prides, they also symbolise the qualities of leadership and responsibility. This encourages individuals to take charge of their healing journey and support others in their struggles. However, Lions do spent a lot of time lying around and in essence represent *'languor'*. Although fictional, Aslan from *The Lion, the Witch and the Wardrobe* embodies leadership, courage, and selfless sacrifice, teaching the value of bravery and standing firm for what is right, particularly in the face of adversity.

Together, lionesses and show how complementary energies, strength and strategy, courage and care, can help individuals navigate grief with resilience, dignity, compassion and power.

Fable | The Power of Feminine Assertion

Lioness lay beneath the shade of a tree, her golden eyes watching over her cubs. Above, Vulture soared, curious about Lioness's role as leader of the pride. "Lioness, you are strong and assertive, yet gentle with your young. How do you balance both?" Vulture asked, swooping lower.

Lioness lifted her head proudly. "Because true strength is rooted in the feminine, Vulture. It's not about domination, but about nurturing, protecting, and guiding with wisdom. The feminine power is fierce yet tender."

Vulture landed on a nearby branch. "But don't you ever need to be aggressive?" Lioness smiled. "Aggression has its place, but assertion comes from a deeper strength. I lead not by force, but by understanding. The feminine knows when to assert itself and when to nurture. In that balance lies true power."

The animals of the savannah saw Lioness not just as a fierce hunter, but as a leader who embodied the wisdom of feminine power. From Lioness, they learned that strength comes from knowing when to protect and when to guide, nurturing life while standing strong.

54
Elephant

Royalty and Strength (9)
The Ancient Power of Royalty

Elephant, aligned with the number 54, embodies ancient power, and the wisdom and compassion of royalty. In your grief journey, Elephant reminds you to honour the legacy of your experiences and trust in the enduring strength that comes from deep wisdom. Like an elephant that remembers its past and carries itself with dignity, you can draw on the power of your inner wisdom to navigate the complex emotions of grief.

* **Opportunity:** Elephant offers you the chance to tap into the ancient wisdom of your ancestors and your soul, grounding you in strength as you process grief.

- **Challenge:** The challenge lies in embracing your inner power without letting the weight of the past overwhelm you.

Questions for today

How can you draw on the wisdom of your past experiences to guide you through your current grief? What compassion and benevolence do you need to bestow on others around you in order for you to move forward yourself? What grounding energy do you need in your life to help transform you as you transition to your next phase? What memories do you need to move forward on to provide compassion and forgiveness? Have you been gullible in your dealings with people? Are you needing to have a perfectionist approach to your life right now and how is that serving you? Where can you demonstrate altruism and support for the greater good? Who can you be of service to?

Affirmation:

- "I honour the ancient wisdom within me as I walk through my grief with dignity."
- "I carry the strength of my ancestors and the wisdom of my spirit."

Self-Care Activity

Reflect on the lessons you've learned from the past. Write down how these lessons can support you in your current healing journey. Write a letter to your future self about how much you are learning right now and how proud you are of yourself. Set a date for when it is to be opened.

Story

Elephants embody wisdom, compassion, and strength across cultures, offering guidance for navigating life's challenges. Their remarkable memory and intelligence teach the value of learning from experience, while their strong social bonds encourage empathy and care for others. As resilient creatures, elephants demonstrate the power of perseverance during difficult times. Their mourning of the dead highlights the importance of honouring loved ones and maintaining connections with ancestors, reminding us to celebrate and cherish those who have passed.

Ganesha, in Hindu mythology is the elephant-headed God, symbolises wisdom, prosperity, and the removal of obstacles. His teachings encourage individuals to embrace their inner strength and overcome challenges in their healing journey.

In African cultures, the elephant represents memory, ancestral wisdom, and leadership within the animal kingdom. Its strong familial bonds, nurturing nature, and majestic presence have made it a symbol of loyalty, protection, and even royalty. Revered for both intelligence and social cohesion, elephants teach the value of community support and the importance of honouring ancestral traditions.

In Buddhism, the white elephant is considered a sacred symbol of purity and enlightenment. This connection emphasises the importance of spiritual growth, reflecting the importance of compassion and mental strength on the path of your healing journey.

Fable | The Ancient Power of Royalty
The great matriarch Elephant moved slowly through the grasslands, her presence commanding respect and quiet awe. She had led her herd through decades of seasons, guiding them with wisdom and care. But time had come, and the herd felt the weight of her failing strength.

One morning, as the sun painted the sky in soft gold, the matriarch took her final rest beneath the ancient trees. The herd gathered, their grief heavy, trumpeting softly in sorrow. Among them, the young matriarch stepped forward, trembling yet determined.

"Do not fear," the elder's memory seemed to whisper through the rustling grass. "The cycles of life continue. My journey ends, but the path remains for those who honour it." The young matriarch lifted her head, feeling both the burden and the blessing of her new role. She remembered her predecessor's lessons: to move with compassion, to balance strength with gentleness, to guide the herd with patience and remembrance for those that had gone before. Though grief lingered, it was also a reminder that life flows in cycles of completion and renewal.

The animals of the grasslands learned that through endings, wisdom is passed, compassion is deepened, and leadership continues. True power is found not only in life, but in the grace of honouring those who have gone before and stepping forward to carry the legacy.

55
Bee

Fertility (55)

The Sweetness of Life's Nectar

Bee, aligned with the number 55, embodies the sweetness of life and the radiant energy of the sun. It reminds you that life's nectar can be found within your own heart. Even in grief, moments of joy and connection can be recognised and gathered. Bee encourages purposeful action and care, showing that focused intention nurtures both yourself and the wider world. Its message is to harvest the richness of life while the sun shines, allowing your spirit to flourish and your days to be fertile with meaning. Bee's lesson is that individual efforts, when aligned with love, contribute to the healing of the whole.

- **Opportunity:** Bee helps you find moments of sweetness and purpose in your grief, showing you how even small acts of care and connection can bring comfort.
- **Challenge:** The challenge is to not become isolated in grief, but to remember the importance of community and collective healing.

Questions for today

How can you find sweetness in the simple moments of life, even as you navigate your grief? Have you been trying to heal alone and now need to return to the 'hive' for comfort and security? Or have you been relying too much on others to provide you comfort and joy, and need to step away to explore your own joys on your new journey? Have you tried to keep busy to avoid your grief? Are you not doing what you want in order to be part of a productive team? Are you feeling restless and wanting to create a new life?

Affirmation:

- "I find sweetness and purpose in the simple moments of life."
- "I honour the connections that nurture me and support my healing."

Self-Care Activity

Share a meaningful conversation or moment with a loved one. Let this connection be a reminder of the sweetness that remains in life. Plant a flower that will attract bees to your garden or balcony. Make a recipe with honey in it.

Story

Bee embodies the qualities of community, hard work, and transformation. The ancient wisdom associated with bee encourages us to navigate grief with diligence and connection to our communities.

Bees thrive in colonies, emphasising the importance of community and collaboration. This teaches individuals to seek support from others during their grief journey. They are known for their industriousness in collecting nectar and producing honey. Their diligence encourages individuals to remain committed to their healing process and put in the necessary effort. The process of turning nectar into honey symbolises transformation and the sweetness that can come from hard work. This teaches individuals that healing often requires time and effort, leading to growth and renewal. Bees play a vital role in pollination, highlighting the interconnectedness of all living beings. This encourages individuals to connect with nature as a source of healing and inspiration.

In Greek mythology, Artemis is associated with bees, particularly in the city of Ephesus, where she was depicted with bee imagery due to her role as a protector and nurturer of the city and its people. Her connection emphasises the importance of nurturing relationships and honouring the cycles of life. Bees were considered sacred in ancient Egypt, symbolising royalty and power. Their teachings emphasise the importance of community and the sweetness of life that can emerge from hardship.

The Bee, with its dedication, organisation, and role in sustaining the hive, teaches us that healing from grief requires patience, cooperation, and steady effort, guiding individuals to rebuild and nurture their lives with resilience and purpose.

Fable | The Sweetness of Life's Nectar
Bee darted through the meadow, her wings a blur of motion, chasing the scent of new blossoms. The garden was alive with constant change—flowers bloomed, wilted, and were replaced by unexpected buds. Bee

thrived in this rhythm, moving swiftly, sensing opportunities, and embracing each shift with curiosity.

"Bee," chirped a Sparrow perched nearby, "how do you keep going when everything keeps changing?"

Bee paused in midair, tasting the golden nectar of a vibrant flower. "Change is where life's sweetness hides," she said. "I cannot cling to the old bloom or fear the wind that scatters petals. Every shift is a chance to discover something new, to taste life's nectar in ways I never imagined."

Sparrow looked doubtful. "But what if the flowers are gone, or the wind is too strong?"

Bee hummed, spinning in the sunlight. "Then I fly differently, explore boldly, adapt quickly. Life is a dance of risk and discovery. The more I embrace movement and uncertainty, the more I uncover its hidden treasures. The nectar is sweetest when we are willing to journey through the unknown."

The animals watched Bee flit tirelessly, her path unpredictable yet purposeful. They realised that embracing adventure, remaining flexible, and trusting in the flow of change brings not only survival but joy. Bee taught them that the world's sweetness is always available to those courageous enough to move with it, to adapt, and to turn uncertainty into opportunity.

56.
Tiger

Passion (11)

The Power of Passion

Tiger, aligned with the number 11, symbolises the raw force of passion and power. In grief, Tiger reminds you to reconnect with the fire of life, even as you move through sorrow. Tiger's lesson is that passion can fuel your healing, giving you the energy and determination to rise again after loss. It encourages you to act with courage and embrace your inner power to transform pain into purpose.

✽ **Opportunity:** Tiger helps you rekindle the passion for life, reminding you that your power lies in your ability to move through grief with intensity and courage.

* **Challenge:** The challenge is to not be consumed by anger or despair, but to channel these powerful emotions into purposeful action.

Questions for today

How can you harness the power of your emotions to fuel your healing journey? Have your moods become more erratic? Do you feel ungrounded and unable to maintain a sense of equilibrium? How can anger drive you forward with action? How can sadness allow you help shape new choices for your future? How can fear open doors to greater self-reflection and empowerment? What will be illuminated in your life as a result of you becoming more passionate and powerful about your life's direction? Are you experiencing anxiety and worry through rumination and overthinking?

Affirmation:
- "I embrace my inner power and passion, using it to transform my grief into strength."
- "I move through grief with courage and intensity, honouring my emotions."

Self-Care Activity

Engage in a physical activity that brings out your inner strength and passion. Whether through movement, art, or expression, let your power flow freely. Play music that has strong beat that can resonate through you.

Story

Tiger embodies the qualities of strength, courage, and independence across various cultures. However, in some places the core word is *cowardice*, demonstrating the need to assert courage and think more clearly about what lies ahead.

Their teachings inspire individuals to embrace their power, confront their fears, and trust their instincts in the healing process. The ancient wisdom associated with tiger encourages us to navigate grief with strength and grace. Tiger, symbolising strength, courage, and independence, carries significant meaning in various cultures. Tigers are apex predators, and the largest in the cat family - representing raw strength and power. They teach individuals to embrace their inner strength and assertiveness, particularly in challenging times. Tigers are known for their fearless nature, symbolising the importance of courage in facing fears. This encourages individuals to confront their grief and the emotions that accompany it. It is also often viewed as an animal spirit that embodies heightened awareness and intuition, guiding individuals to trust their inner wisdom and personal journey.

In Chinese medicine, the Tiger embodies courage, strength, and vitality, reflecting the liver's role in ensuring the smooth flow of qi and blood throughout the body. Its energy teaches resilience, assertiveness, and the importance of standing in one's power while maintaining balance and harmony.

In Hindu mythology, Lord Shiva is often depicted with a tiger or riding one, symbolising his power and mastery over nature. This connection emphasises the importance of harnessing inner strength during the healing journey. In Chinese culture, the tiger is a symbol of bravery and strength. Those born in the Year of the Tiger are believed to embody these qualities, teaching individuals to embrace their inherent power.

Many Indigenous cultures, particularly in India, view tigers as symbols of strength and independence. Their teachings highlight the importance of standing strong in the face of adversity and honouring one's personal journey.

Tigers are solitary creatures, representing self-reliance and independence, reminding individuals to trust themselves and their instincts while navigating their healing journey. Tigers exhibit a balance of fierce strength and graceful movement, teaching the importance of finding harmony between power and gentleness in the healing process.

Fable | The Power of Passion
Tiger prowled silently through the jungle, its striped coat blending with the shadows. Deer, grazing nearby, watched warily but didn't flee. "Tiger, you move with such intensity and focus. Where does your power come from?" Deer asked, curious.

Tiger's amber eyes gleamed as it spoke. "My power comes from passion, Deer. Every step, every breath, every hunt is filled with purpose and energy. I live with intensity because I am driven by the fire within me."

Deer tilted its head. "But doesn't passion make you reckless?" Tiger smiled. "No, Deer. Passion, when guided by wisdom, is the source of true strength. It fuels me, gives me the courage to face challenges, and the drive to pursue my dreams. Without passion, there is no power."

The animals admired Tiger's fierce spirit, understanding that passion, when channelled wisely, was a force of creation and transformation. From Tiger, they learned that to live fully, they must embrace the fire within, using it to fuel their journey with purpose and strength.

INDEX ON PYTHAGOREAN NUMBERS & ANIMALS

A quick guide to the core meanings of each number.

1. Individuality & New Beginnings / Co-dependency & Selfishness | **Eagle, Turtle, Buffalo, Armadillo, Antelope, Raccoon**
   - **Higher expression:** Initiative, courage, pioneering spirit, taking charge of life and decisions.
   - **Challenge side:** Ego, stubbornness, or putting personal ambition above others.

2. Partnership & Sensitivity / Insecurity & Dependence | **Hawk, Mouse**
   - **Higher expression:** Cooperation, diplomacy, emotional awareness, nurturing relationships.
   - **Challenge side:** Over-sensitivity, passivity, or reliance on others for validation.

3. Expression & Joy / Blocked expression & Superficiality | **Elk, Porcupine, Owl, Rabbit, Swan, Wild Boar**
   - **Higher expression:** Expressiveness, optimism, inspiration, artistic and social creativity.
   - **Challenge side:** Scattered energy, superficiality, gossip, avoidance of deeper responsibilities.

4. Stability & Foundation / Self-Limiting & Rigidity | **Deer, Coyote, Turkey, Dolphin, Salmon**
   - **Higher expression:** Organisation, practicality, reliability, building solid foundations.
   - **Challenge side:** Inflexibility, resistance to change, or feeling trapped by routine.

5. Change & Freedom / Excessive & Restlessness | **Bear, Dog, Opossum, Ant, Whale, Alligator**
   - **Higher expression:** Adaptability, curiosity, embracing change, seeking growth and variety.
   - **Challenge side:** Impulsiveness, unpredictability, or difficulty committing to long-term goals.

6. Nurturing & Responsibility / Victimhood & Overbearing | **Snake, Wolf, Crow, Bat, Jaguar**
   - **Higher expression:** Nurturing, service, protecting family and community, creating balance.
   - **Challenge side:** Over-involvement, controlling tendencies, or self-sacrifice to excess.

7. Introspection & Wisdom / Disconnected & Isolated | **Skunk, Raven, Fox, Grouse, Spider, Black Panther**
   - **Higher expression:** Spiritual awareness, analysis, contemplation, deep understanding.
   - **Challenge side:** Withdrawal, secrecy, or overthinking that blocks action.

8. Power & Abundance / Dominance & Disempowerment | **Otter, Mountain Lion, Squirrel, Horse, Lion/Lioness**
    - **Higher expression:** Authority, success, management of resources, achieving material and personal goals, loyalty and generosity.
    - **Challenge side:** Greed, control issues, misuse of power, materialism, consumerism.

9. Completion & Compassion / Martyrdom & Unforgiving| **Butterfly, Lynx, Dragonfly, Lizard, Blue Heron, Elephant**
    - **Higher expression:** Compassion, humanitarianism, closure, embracing the bigger picture.
    - **Challenge side:** Self-sacrifice, overextension, or difficulty letting go.

11. Intuition & Illumination / Anxiety & Overwhelm | **Moose, Badger, Frog, Prairie Dog, Tiger**
    - **Higher expression:** Spiritual insight, inspiration, illumination, heightened intuition, guiding others with vision.
    - **Challenge side:** Anxiety, self-doubt, nervous tension, or oversensitivity when overwhelmed by inner gifts.

22. Master Builder & Manifestation / Control & Overextension | **Beaver**
    - **Higher expression:** Practical mastery, building lasting foundations, turning dreams into reality, creating structures that benefit many.
    - **Challenge side:** Feeling overwhelmed by responsibility, perfectionism, or struggling to balance vision with practicality.

33. Master Teacher & Compassion / Self-sacrifice & Burden | **Weasel**
    - **Higher expression:** Unconditional love, teaching through service, inspiring others to grow, embodying compassion in action.
    - **Challenge side:** Self-sacrifice to excess, feeling burdened by the needs of others, or neglecting personal boundaries.

44. Master Healer & Practical Wisdom / Rigidity & Exhaustion | **Hummingbird**
    - **Higher expression:** Strategic problem-solving, healing through knowledge and action, creating sustainable impact, grounded wisdom.
    - **Challenge side:** Stubbornness, inflexibility, or misuse of power when structure becomes rigidity.

55. The Sweetness of Life's Nectar / Restlessness & Impulsiveness | **Bee**
    - **Higher expression:** Freedom, adventure, transformative energy, embracing change, finding joy in life's experiences.
    - **Challenge side:** Impulsiveness, restlessness, inconsistency, or resisting necessary change.

CULTURAL AND SOURCE ACKNOWLEDGEMENT

This book draws inspiration from a range of cultural and spiritual traditions that use animals as symbols of protection, wisdom, healing, and transformation. In particular, it builds on widely recognised sources such as:

- *Animal Medicine Cards* by Jamie Sams and David Carson (Santa Fe: Bear & Company, 1988)
- *Animal Speak* by Ted Andrews (Llewellyn Publications, 1993)
- *Animal Dreaming* by Scott Alexander King (New Holland Publishers, Australia, 2006).
- *Animal Spirit Guides: An Easy-to-Use Handbook for Identifying and Understanding Your Power Animals and Animal Spirit Helpers* by Steven D. Farmer (Crossing Press 2005)

These works explore how animals guide reflection, offer practical lessons, and support emotional and spiritual growth.

In addition to animal symbolism, the book is informed by seminal publications on grief, personal growth, spiritual practice and the human experience of loss. Key texts include:

- **Elisabeth Kübler-Ross's** *On Death and Dying* (1969) and *The Human Encounter with Death* edited by C. Denis (1981), which delve into the stages of grief and the transformative potential of facing mortality.

- **Neale Donald Walsch's key books**, including *Conversations with God* (1995), *Conversations with God, Book 2* (1997), *Conversations with God, Book 3* (1998), and *Home with God: In a Life That Never Ends* (2006), offer spiritual dialogue that challenges conventional beliefs and encourages personal reflection.
- **Dan Millman's** works, including *Way of the Peaceful Warrior* (1980) and *The Life You Were Born to Live* (1993), explore the integration of physical, emotional, and spiritual growth through personal stories, practical guidance, and the discovery of one's life purpose.
- **Caroline Myss's** *Archetypes: Who Are You?* (2013), exploring the universal patterns of behaviour that shape our identities and life paths.
- **Tony Robbins's** *Unlimited Power* (1986) and *Awaken the Giant Within* (1991), providing tools for personal empowerment and transformation.
- **Ann Moura's** *Green Witchcraft* series (1996 - 2003), blending folk magic, fairy lore, and herb craft to connect with the natural world and its rhythms.
- **Dr. Joe Dispenza's** *Breaking the Habit of Being Yourself* (2012) and *Becoming Supernatural* (2017), integrating neuroscience and quantum physics to facilitate healing and change.
- **Rupi Kaur's** *Healing Through Words* (2022) offers a collection of guided poetry writing exercises designed to help readers explore themes of trauma, loss, heartache, love, family, healing, and self-celebration.
- **Esther Hicks's** *Ask and It Is Given* (2004), *The Law of Attraction* (2006), and *The Astonishing Power of Emotions* (2008), focusing

on the principles of manifestation and emotional guidance.
- **John Edward's** *One Last Time* (1998) and *Crossing Over* (2001), offering insights into mediumship and the continuity of consciousness.
- **Thom F. Cavalli's** *Alchemical Psychology* (2002), merging Jungian psychology with alchemical symbolism to understand the psyche.
- **Diane Stein's** *The Women's Book of Healing* (1994), a guide to holistic practices for women's health and well-being.
- **Deepak Chopra's** *The Book of Secrets* (2004), offering insights into the mysteries of life and consciousness.
- **Graham Travis's** *Colour Healing* (1989), exploring the therapeutic use of colour in healing practices.
- **Richard Moss MD's** *The Mandala of Being* (2004), examining the relationship between consciousness and emotional healing.
- **Lucia Capacchione's** *The Art of Emotional Healing* (1991), utilising creative expression as a means of emotional release and healing.
- **Neil Koelmeyer and Ursula Kolecki's** *The Secret Language of Your Name* (2005), interpreting the vibrational significance of names.
- **Inna Segal's** *The Secret Language of Your Body* (2009), decoding the messages of the body to understand emotional and physical health.

I also wish to acknowledge the influence of personal teachers and mentors whose guidance shaped the approach of this book, as well as cultural and spiritual wisdom that informed its development. A special nod goes to Matthew McConaughey's *Greenlights* (2020) for giving me the push I needed to bring this book over the line.

Together, these influences form a framework that blends practical, psychological, and spiritual approaches, emphasising reflection, connection, and the lessons we can learn from both the natural world and the human experience.

The content herein is not intended to represent or reproduce any specific Indigenous, religious, or cultural knowledge system, but rather to respectfully interpret and adapt symbolic insights for personal reflection and grief recovery.

I also acknowledge and pay my deepest respects to the past, present, and future Traditional Custodians and Elders of this great nation. I honour their enduring connection to land, waters, language, and spirit, and recognise them as the keepers of memory, culture, and spiritual well-being. I acknowledge the profound wisdom and guidance they continue to provide, sustaining and inspiring generations.

Reproduction

No part of *A New Way to Live With Loss* may be reproduced, stored, or transmitted in any form or by any means, electronic, mechanical, photocopying, recording, or otherwise, without the prior written permission of Hembury Books. Excerpts or quotations may be used for review, commentary, educational, or research purposes only when properly cited, including the author's name, title, and publisher. For all other uses, including reproduction, adaptation, or distribution, please contact Hembury Books directly for written permission

www.ingramcontent.com/pod-product-compliance
Lightning Source LLC
Chambersburg PA
CBHW020402080526
44584CB00014B/1142